Asking Questions About Behavior

AN INTRODUCTION
TO WHAT PSYCHOLOGISTS DO
SECOND EDITION

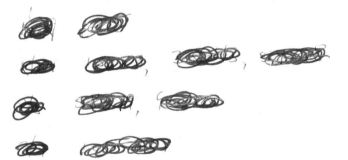

Asking Questions About Behavior

AN INTRODUCTION
TO WHAT PSYCHOLOGISTS DO
SECOND EDITION

MICHAEL E. DOHERTY and KENNETH M. SHEMBERG
Bowling Green State University

Scott, Foresman and Company • **Glenview, Illinois**
Dallas, Tex. • Oakland, N. J. • Palo Alto, Cal. •
Tucker, Ga. • London, England

Library of Congress Cataloging in Publication Data

Doherty, Michael E.   1935-
  Asking questions about behavior.

  Bibliography: p.
  1. Psychology.   2. Psychological research.   I. Shemberg, Kenneth M., joint
author.   II. Title.
BF121.D59   1978   150   77-20856
ISBN 0-673-15043-7

12345678910-GBC-858483828180797877

A Letter to the Student

very year students sign up for an introductory psychology course eagerly hoping to find out why they feel and act as they do and what makes people tick. They expect psychology to help provide them with answers to questions of how they can be more effective, happier people. Before the end of the term, many students are disappointed and disillusioned, looking elsewhere for the answers to *real-life* questions that they had thought psychology could provide. They see little reason for learning about reflex arcs, standard deviations, and the behavior of rats. They sometimes feel cheated, and many never take another course in psychology.

We believe that such disillusionment is unnecessary. Psychologists are so used to the necessity for precision and careful controls in research that they assume the need is self-evident to everyone. They forget the long, slow road they traveled to arrive at their convictions and enthusiasms. In this Second Edition of *Asking Questions About Behavior*, we want to help you along this road. We want to help you understand the process of research and to show you how the methods of psychological investigation can relate to the many questions you have brought to your psychology course.

Part I begins with a list of questions many of our students have asked on the first day of their introductory psychology class. From this list we focus on a two-part "grand question": Why does one's personality change when under stress? How can psychologists help? After asking the question, we show what happens when we try to answer it. We analyze it word by word to see if it is answerable. We discuss why it is not answerable as it is posed, and we go on to examine the requirements of an answerable question.

In Part II, we move to the more specific, answerable questions that are a part of the grand question. Here we look at a variety of research studies, each focusing on one question that deals with the relationship between stress and personality. Included are Hunt's study of a Freudian hypothesis concerning childhood stress, Brady's study of ulcers in "executive" monkeys, Schachter's work on the relationship between stress and the tendency to seek closeness to other people, Miller's classic study demonstrating how situations can become stressful, Shurley's investigation of the effects of sensory deprivation and isolation, Masserman's work with experimental neuroses in animals, Johnson's study of the role of physiological arousal in experimental neuroses, Cannon's fascinating attempt to analyze the mechanisms responsible for voodoo deaths, and a case of a severely disturbed boy in whom glasses-wearing behavior was established and tantrum behavior was extinguished by behavior modification techniques.

In this Second Edition, we have added studies to show an even wider variety of research methods. New to this edition are a look by Balke and his colleagues at management-labor negotiations, Davidson's laboratory study and Silverman and Geer's clinical study of the use of systematic desensitization in reducing phobias, and Budzynski's research on the effect of biofeedback in reducing tension headaches. As in the First Edition, all these studies are told in a narrative, nontechnical style. In each case we try to point out both what was learned and what questions were *not* answered by the study.

The studies that we have selected reflect only a handful of the thousands of published psychological investigations. We used three general guidelines in our selection:

1. *The studies must relate to the grand question but they must differ from one another.* We hope to give you a feeling for the magnitude of the grand question, as well as a feeling for the breadth of psychology. Thus, though the selections may at first appear to be a hodgepodge of unrelated reports, we hope to communicate the diversity *and* the potential interrelatedness of many of the apparently unconnected subfields of psychology.

2. *The studies must illustrate important issues about the process of research.* With this purpose in mind, our goal is not to present current psychological data but rather to present the diverse methods of seeking data. As such, the recency of the studies was a minor guideline; you will find some new and some "classical" studies, all chosen for what they can tell us about the *process* of psychological investigation.

3. *The studies must be interesting.* We believe that if scientific psychology is clearly presented, the insights that follow make it intrinsically interesting. We have tried, however, to avoid the tendency of psychologists to find almost any carefully conducted study of interest! Instead, we have tried to highlight the question behind each study and the answer it gives, or the additional questions it raises, that can bring more light to the grand question.

Finally, in Part III, we are ready to pull together some of the specific points made in Part II and present some major concepts, principles, and issues basic to psychological research. This section has been greatly expanded in the Second Edition to include a broader discussion of experimental methods and the controversies surrounding them, including expanded sections on ethical considerations, generalizability, and replication in both laboratory and clinical research.

By starting out in pursuit of answers to questions important to students like yourself, we will try to lead you back, step by step, to an appreciation of the complexity and precision involved in asking and answering questions about behavior.

M. E. D.
K. M. S.

Contents

Asking Questions About Behavior

AN INTRODUCTION
TO WHAT PSYCHOLOGISTS DO

SECOND EDITION

Part I Asking Questions

INTRODUCTION

Introductory psychology textbooks are almost always organized so that they progress from specific to more general topics. The basic assumption underlying this order is that the more complex areas of the study of psychology, like personality and social psychology, can only be understood if we understand more basic processes like learning, motivation, and perception. Thus, the reasoning goes, only if you first grasp the laws governing the elements will you be able to understand the more complex aspects of behavior.

There are many good reasons for writing beginning psychology textbooks in this fashion. However, we believe that the presentation of psychology in the pattern described above can be misleading in one respect. While such a presentation may organize the field in a logically and psychologically meaningful way, it does not truly reflect what a psychologist does. It is likely to leave you with an inaccurate picture of the maturity of psychology as a scientific discipline, and with a false impression of the extent to which the goals of the science of psychology are clearly defined. It would be good for you to know at the very outset of your studies that scientific psychology is very young and that its goals are not well defined.

Not too long ago psychologists were attempting to develop theories that were very broad and that would enable them to explain all aspects of behavior. We will refer to these systems as "grand theories of behavior." Some psychologists are now engaged in the development of smaller, less grand theories to explain much more limited aspects of behavior. Others are not seeking to develop theories at all. Virtually all psychologists who do research have now abandoned the pursuit of the Holy Grail of grand behavior theory. All psychologists are certainly interested in the totality of behavior and would unquestionably like to understand the totality of behavior. But the impossibility of doing so right now is forced upon us by the enormous complexity of the interrelationships between the environment and the person. At any given moment, literally billions of events occur within us and between us and the environment. Thus researchers often devote themselves to one of the "simpler" phenomena, such as learning, motivation, or perception. But these, too, are incredibly complicated, and the body of data available from the research studies that relate to any one of them staggers the imagination. So in actual practice a psychologist studies intensively some small aspect of one of the so-called simpler behavioral phenomena, hoping to discover the knowledge necessary to understand some small piece of the environment-organism interaction. There is as yet no Einstein on the horizon of scientific psychology who gives promise of constructing the psychological counterpart of relativity theory!

If contemporary psychologists are not attempting to construct all-inclusive theories of behavior, what are they doing? What is the goal that provides the motivation for the many studies you will find in your text? That is the question to which this book is addressed. Why do psychologists do the kinds of things they do? Why do they ask the kinds of questions they ask? Why does one ask, for example, Will depriving a very young rat of food affect the rat's later behavior? when you, the student, have so many seemingly more interesting and important questions you'd like to have answered?

ASKING IMPORTANT QUESTIONS

he list of questions below includes some of the replies given by students on the first day of a class in introductory psychology when they were asked what question about human behavior they would most like answered by a course in psychology.

How much influence does environment have on personality development?

Can a chemical imbalance in one's system affect the unconscious mind, and if so, can it be detected through behavior?

What possesses a person to act like an authority about a subject even though he or she may know nothing about the subject?

How much influence do parents actually have on their children's ideas of life?

Why are people prejudiced toward other people?

Why do people purposefully humiliate and physically harm their loved ones, even though they are aware of the emotional and bodily harm that results from their actions?

Why is something a fear stimulus for one person and not another?

What are the psychological "causes" or theories for the development of a subculture, such as a juvenile gang or a street-corner society?

What are the determining factors that make up a "stable" person and what are the limits to stability?

What causes some people to become very hot-headed and blow up into a temper tantrum?

Why does one's personality change under stress? How can psychologists help?

These are all "good" questions, some dealing with issues of great personal relevance, others with issues of overbearing social importance. It is very possible that you are beginning this course in psychology with similar questions. It is also quite possible that neither the questions above nor the questions you are entertaining will be answered by your beginning course. They cannot be answered because the questions as posed above are not asked in a form that allows a scientist to investigate them; they are not scientific questions. The question, Does motivation influence perception? may appear to be a scientific question, perhaps more so than the students' questions because of the wording. But under a closer analysis you will find that the only reasonable answer to the question as stated is, "Yes and no—it depends upon what the questioner means by motivation, by influence, and by perception."

To be sure, many questions will be posed in your course, and many will be answered. But they will be less grand and perhaps less exciting to you than you may wish. Many of us who have chosen the science of behavior as our life's work began our study in psychology with similar unanswerable questions. These questions provided considerable motivation for study, and sooner or later in our development as psychologists we picked one out to focus upon, to try to answer. But once we began to attack our question, we immediately faced a number of problems common to all researchers, problems forcing the investigator to recast the question in terms that allow some hope of finding an answer. One of these problems is that of *definition*. The scientist must define terms so that the definition is precise; that is, it includes just what it should, but excludes everything else. The definition must be clear enough so that other people know what it means and broad enough to be sufficiently important to warrant investigation.

Attempts to develop such definitions almost always involve cutting the original question down to manageable proportions, or more frequently, cutting it up into several smaller questions, or more frequently still, discovering that several other preliminary questions must be answered first. It is not at all uncommon to see an investigator shift the focus of interest and become permanently involved in trying to answer one of the narrower or preliminary questions.

The problem of definition is no simple one, as every reader who has ever been involved in an argument with a good debater knows. It is often used as a last-ditch defense by someone who does not wish to expend the effort involved in thinking or working, as when a person argues that there is no point in studying juvenile delinquency because no one even agrees on what juvenile delinquency is! However, it is necessary to deal with the problem of definition if we are to answer questions in a scientific manner. *With respect to the quest for a scientific understanding of behavior, clear definition of terms is crucial.* But you should not conclude falsely from this discussion that research questions in psychology are merely matters of definition. While psychologists do in fact grapple with problems of definition all the time, and define terms with exquisite care, such definition is only the first step toward answering a research question.

To illustrate the above, but primarily to communicate to you a feeling for why psychologists do the kinds of things they do, we have selected one two-part question from the students' questions presented at the beginning of this section and tried to "answer" it.

ASKING ANSWERABLE QUESTIONS

hy does one's personality change under stress? How can psychologists help?

Clearly, this is an important question. It has implications for the behavior of people in riot-torn streets, people at war, people driving cars on busy highways, children being scolded by their parents, students taking exams, women in childbirth—in short, for the behavior of people under the limitless number of environmental conditions we call *stress*. But let us emphasize a critical point that has already been mentioned above:

The question as posed cannot be investigated scientifically.

Before a question can be considered scientifically meaningful, it must be asked in such a fashion that a scientist can make the *observations* necessary to answer it. Those observations must have certain characteristics to be acceptable as scientifically valid. They must be observations of situations that are relevant to the question—that is, situations that constitute stress and behaviors that constitute some aspect of personality change. The observations must be of stimulus situations, environmental conditions, or whatever you may wish to call them, that reasonable people would agree are within the meaning of stress. Some specific aspect or aspects of behavior, some set of observable responses, are selected for observation to provide a basis for deciding whether anything like personality change occurs. In order for the research to be scientifically meaningful, the observations must be made under carefully *controlled* conditions and must be *objective* in nature. We will provide many examples of control and objective observation in Part II, and we will explore them further in Part III. Let us define them carefully here, and briefly discuss them.

The word *control* has several meanings in science, but all of those meanings seem to have a common core. That core is that control serves to rule out as many explanations of the events being studied as possible. Casual observations in the natural environment suffer from the fact that potentially significant aspects of the environment are all varying simultaneously with the behavior. They are all entangled together, or *confounded*. It is difficult, if not impossible, to identify which events caused the behavior, which events were caused by the behavior, and which events were unrelated to the behavior. One meaning of the word *control* speaks directly to this problem and is referred to as experimental control. *Experimental control* refers to the practice of holding all potential environmental influences on behavior constant, except those which the scientist is investigating. In a psychological experiment, the investigator *manipulates* systematically, or changes, some potential influences in the environment; then the investigator carefully observes whether the behavior of interest also changes systematically. If it does, then it can be argued that the manipulation caused the behavior to change, since everything else has been held constant. A closely related meaning of control is in the use of the term *control group*. If an experimenter manipulates some aspect of the environment, keeps everything else constant, and observes that the behavior of the subjects in the experimental group changes, what does the change mean? What is it compared with? In many, many psychological experiments the comparison is with a group treated identically with the experimental group, *except* in this group the aspect of the environment has not been manipulated. What an obvious idea! But it took so long in the evolution of scientific knowledge to develop! That comparison group is called the control group. A third meaning refers to the control that any scientist, experimenter, or observer exercises over the conditions of observation, but that really brings up the concept of *objectivity*.

Objectivity must surely be one of the most misunderstood and maligned concepts in science. People who do not understand the scientific method are likely to say that objectivity is impossible, that after all it is a person making and interpreting scientific observation and that all people have biases. That objection is true only if you misunderstand what scientists mean by objectivity. Objectivity simply means that a given observation can be agreed upon by independent observers. No more. No less. If you were to send two observers into a classroom and instruct them to rate a child on "hostility," you may well expect to get two very different ratings. The term *hostility* is open to many different interpretations. So the observations would not be very objective. On the other hand, suppose you instructed the observers to count the number of times that a particular child punched or hit other children, defined what you meant by punched or hit, maybe showed the observers a training film to sharpen the definition, and *then* turned them loose to make the observation. You would very likely get very high agreement among the observers. That's objectivity. Reading measurements from a dial—that's objectivity, because different observers get almost exactly the same readings. In fact, the neatest, shortest definition of objectivity that we know is "interobserver agreement." That's what the term *objectivity* boils down to—*the extent to which different observers agree on what happened.* Not on what it *means.* Not on whether it's *good* or *bad.* Just *what happened.* Scientists use all sorts of elaborate aids to assure objectivity. The observations are made under highly controlled conditions, often with the help of elaborate apparatus. The use of the apparatus often ensures that objective observations may be made by more than one observer.

The concepts described in the above paragraphs represent the essence of science. When we claim to have the answer to any important question about behavior, we should be able to answer the question, Where is the evidence? If we cannot produce the evidence in the form of objective observations of the behavior, observations that have been made under carefully controlled conditions, our answer cannot be considered scientific. It may be poetic or philosophical. It may or may not be a good answer—but whatever it may be, it is not a *scientific* answer.

Let us briefly summarize what has just been stated, and then begin to look carefully at what is involved when a scientist goes about answering questions about the effect of stress on personality.

In order for a question to be answered scientifically, it must be asked so that objective observations of all significant items in the question can be made under controlled conditions.

The above is absolutely crucial to your understanding of the science of psychology. It is the rock on which the "big" questions founder, but also the rock on which contemporary science is built. A close analysis of our student's question about stress, personality, and how psychologists can help will make the above crucial statement more meaningful and will also help us make the question more meaningful. We will look at the key words of the student's question, one by one, in an effort to explain why the question as posed is unanswerable. By exploring the implications of *each* term in that question, we will attempt to show why it is necessary to reduce that big question to many smaller ones.

Why. Scientists are curious people. They ask about the "why" of things all the time. But when they set about asking answerable questions, the "why" is dropped. Actually if the "why" question is about ultimate causality (Why is there life on earth?), then it would be unscientific, since such questions are in the realm of philosophy or religion. On the other hand, if the "why" is just shorthand for, What is the relationship between . . . or, Under what conditions . . ., then the question could be a legitimate, scientific question, provided the other terms in the question meet the test of observability.

Personality.   Personality is not purple! Nor is it red, yellow, blue, or pink; square, sweet, loud, or hard. It is not an it. Personality is an idea that caught on some time in the history of our language. No one ever saw it, smelled it, tasted it, heard it, or touched it. If someone tries to sell you some at $2.98 per pound, he or she ought to be locked up. If you buy some, you ought to be! Personality is not an it but an idea that has caught on. It has caught on because the idea of personality has helped people make sense out of their own behavior and the behavior of people around them. In some respects the concept of personality is like the concept of force in physics or valence in chemistry. In the terminology of the philosophy of science these ideas are called *hypo-* *thetical constructs*. These constructs—force, valence, gravity, personality—are themselves unobservable; they help us make sense out of our observable world. They help us understand the countless events constantly occurring about us. These constructs enable us to bring some order and simplicity to the complexity that the environment constantly presents to our millions of sense receptors. Constructs themselves vary, however, in their level of scientific rigor.

Personality is a construct that helps us understand consistency in behavior of a person. It also helps us understand differences in behavior among different people. For example, when we refer to a particular person as "basically honest," we are referring to an aspect of personality that supposedly cuts across a variety of different situations, and we are also implying a difference between that person and other people—people whom we would *not* call "basically honest." People frequently use a personality characteristic, such as honesty, as though it were something inside the individual that explains, makes sense out of, or even causes some of the person's observable behavior. In other words, a variety of external, observable behaviors get labeled with a concept that refers to some hypothetical, internal, unobservable process. This makes the behavior seem somehow less complex, less mysterious, and more understandable. It is important to note that while personality can be considered one of these unobservable, hypothetical constructs, it is not a scientifically well-defined construct. It is almost always defined only by behaviors—that is, by the supposed consequences of the construct. Ideally, as we will soon see, constructs should be defined not only by consequences, but by antecedents as well. Personality is a useful term in our everyday vocabulary. It is an idea that has caught on because it has been useful. We can use the term meaningfully in our everyday vocabulary because everyone roughly knows what it means. In order for the term *personality* to have scientific usefulness beyond our everyday understanding, we must specify clearly those observable behaviors that investigators have used as measures of personality—those behaviors to which the concept, or construct, is considered to refer.

The reasoning may seem tortured, but it is not. The word *personality* was "created" sometime long ago to help make sense out of events people saw—out of observables. The everyday use of the word indicates that people roughly agree on the meaning of the word. If we believe that the term may be scientifically useful as well and if we wish to use it in a scientific context, we must employ the observables, or some of them, to which personality refers.

Therefore, we must look at those behaviors considered to be represented by the construct of personality; that is, behaviors that differentiate people from one another and behaviors that can be considered characteristic of given individuals. We must now define personality in terms of observable behavior so that we can make the question a scientifically answerable one. However, as was implied above, the idea of personality represents many behaviors, and no researcher could possibly investigate all of these various meanings of personality. Therefore, what is done is to select one (occasionally two or three) of these indexes of personality for the purpose of making scientific investigation possible. This cuts the question to manageable proportions.

Let's bring this to a more concrete level. A partial list of the observable measures of behavior with which different investigators have defined personality or some aspect of personality should illustrate the point.

Responses to inkblot tests
Responses to a test of anxiety
Breathing rate
Heart rate
How many electric shocks one person will deliver to another
What intensity of electric shock one person will deliver to another
How much shock a person can tolerate
Pupillary dilation
Sweating
Punching a stand-up rubber clown
Memory tasks
Content of stories to ambiguous pictures
Solution of anagrams
Performance on a verbal learning task
Time it takes a person to free-associate
Attitudes expressed toward strangers on a test
Color preference
Job preferences
Judgments of facial expressions of others
Judgments of others' speech
Quality of speech
Susceptibility to group pressure
Rapidity of eyeblink conditioning
Content of dreams

Frequency of dreams
Estimation of size of "threatening" objects
Perceptual distortion
Ratings of personality by peers
Ratings of personality by parents
Self-ratings of personality
Judgments by psychiatrists or psychotherapists
Activity of children at play
Analysis of paintings
Hypnotizability

One or more of the above definitions would be selected by a particular investigator to measure personality. The choice would depend upon the specific interests of the investigator and would be made to suit the purposes of a given investigation. Whatever specific index is selected, two closely related points should be kept in mind:

(1) The original richness and grandeur of the term *personality* are lost—sacrificed—to the rule of rigorous, objective observation under carefully controlled conditions. No longer are we talking about personality with all of the lush associations that have been tied to it through use in novels, films, TV, theories such as psychoanalysis, and everyday speech.

(2) The questions themselves have changed profoundly. They are no longer dealing with the complex, global concept of personality, but are typically dealing with one measure of one aspect of personality.

Change.   Again, everyone knows what the word *change* means. But remember that in a scientific context each word in a research question must be defined not only so that observations can be made, but also so that other investigators can make these objective observations. To do research concerning personality, the construct, personality, must be defined in terms of observables. When we talk about observed changes in personality, these changes must be specified so that someone else can observe the same changes. Most psychologists strive to specify their concepts quantitatively. One of the most important reasons for doing so is that only after we have assigned numbers to a particular aspect of behavior is it possible to address objectively the question of how much or how many. Only by answering how much or how many can we communicate most clearly what we mean by change. Consider the difference between "the subject's personality changed" and "the subject's heart rate increased from seventy to ninety beats per minute." The first report is phrased in nonquantitative terminology; the second, in quantitative units of behavior.

Quantification is not always so easily achieved as implied by the example of counting heartbeats. Even the seemingly clear example of heartbeats per minute may have more to it than meets the eye. If the investigator is using the number of beats per minute as a measure of cardiac activity, that's sensible. It is one direct measure of the quantity in question. But suppose an investigator takes heartbeats per minute as a measure of anxiety? That sort of makes sense—but just sort of. Does heart rate measure anxiety—and only anxiety? Often there is a serious question as to the extent to which the numbers actually measure what the investigator is interested in. The problems involved in assigning numbers usefully to situations and to behaviors are often subtle and complex. Such problems are common in psychological research and are referred to as problems of *measurement*. A discussion of measurement, which is the assignment of numerals to observables (or some characteristics of observables), could have been raised in several places above. Certainly it is relevant to the problem of definition. It could easily have been raised in connection with the difficulties of quantifying personality characteristics. It seems easier, however, to think about the necessity of measurement and the desirability of quantification in terms of the description of change. Change can be described verbally, but it is more convenient and, believe it or not, simpler and more meaningful to describe change quantitatively.

Let's look at another example. We might say: This medication has reduced the student's anxiety; the student now does better on examinations. This verbal description does not specify exactly what was done to induce change. Nor does it clearly state just what changes have occurred. Quantifying this statement presents the issues more clearly and precisely. For example, we might rephrase the outcome as follows: Six weeks of taking 10 milligrams of Librium (a tranquilizer) three times a day has reduced the stress of taking examinations to the extent that the student's grade point average has improved 1.5 points. Numbers specify more clearly changes in *degree* and also changes in the *number* of elements (such as people or responses). Change can also be conceptualized in terms of "direction." That is, change can be for the better or for the worse. In considering our student's question about personality "changing" under stress, it seemed clear that change referred to *negative* effects of stress, effects that are undesirable to the person. Thus, in the remainder of the text, we will be discussing research that investigated undesirable effects of stress.

Stress. People use the term *stress* in many ways. For psychologists, stress is often used to refer to an unobservable, hypothetical construct, a postulated state of the organism that supposedly comes about because of some observable condition in the environment. This state is then assumed to influence behavior. For example, how might we explain why a soldier runs away during a battle? It might be argued that the sights and sounds of combat have produced intolerable stress *in the soldier,* and this internal "state of the organism" *caused* him to run from his position. Other soldiers in the same battle who did not run are presumed, for one reason or another, not to have been in the state of stress to the same degree or are presumed to have developed responses to cope with stress other than running away. Notice, when we use stress as a hypothetical, internal state, we have defined the construct in terms of the situation (the sights and sounds of combat) *and* the behavior (running away). In this usage of stress as a construct, a variety of environmental events, called *stressors*, may produce an internal state of the organism, called *stress*, which in turn causes various forms of disruption of behavior. Scientific constructs are often (and generally should be) defined in terms of antecedent conditions (stimuli) *and* consequences (the resulting behavior). From the point of view of the classical work by Selye (1956) on stress, this internal state of the organism may also be detected by measures of physiological changes.

Another way in which psychologists often use the word *stress* is to consider the term a label that summarizes a wide variety of stimulus situations which have one thing in common—they disrupt the organism. The situations produce maladaptive behaviors; they cause physiological damage; they produce "changes in personality." Notice that in using the term in this way, stress *may* be considered simply as a class of stimulus situations. No reference needs to be made to an internal state. Or the term may be considered to be antecedent to different, unobservable, presumed states of the organism (e.g., fear, frustration, anger, conflict). These are themselves hypothetical constructs. They might be measured by some of those behaviors described above as indexes of personality.

The list of potential situations that constitute stress is endless, but the following examples should give you a good idea of the range of stimuli considered as stress.

A long, loud noise
An unhappy marriage
Combat
An examination
Unavoidable electric shock
Threat of physical harm
Physical harm
Angry parents
Prolonged deprivation of bodily needs
Bodily illness
Solitary confinement
The memory of a guilt-provoking act
Having one's hand plunged into icewater
Motion pictures of automobile accidents
Motion pictures of operations
Threat of failure
Failure

Extreme heat
Extreme cold
Attacks on one's self-esteem
Insults
Being required to solve arithmetic problems rapidly
Combat training
Parachute jumps
Prolonged submersion in a submarine
Waiting for a dentist
Lying on a cart being wheeled to an operating room
Strong, unpleasant odors
Very bright lights
Films of primitive sexual rites
Threat to social status
Snakes
Having rubber snakes dangled in front of you

But you could reasonably ask the question, How do you know that a given situation does produce disruption? If you were going to conduct an experiment on how stress affects some aspect of personality, how would you select an appropriate stimulus situation?

For a stimulus to qualify as stress, it must be capable of disrupting a wide range of behaviors or producing a wide range of negative behavioral consequences. Prolonged or repeated electric shock qualifies. We know from experimentation that if we give electric shocks of certain duration and intensities to humans or animals, the shock will interfere with or disrupt many kinds of adaptive behavior. Thus a proper way for investigators to select the stimulus is to rely upon previous research findings that demonstrate that a given situation disrupts behaviors or produces a variety of negative responses.

What does all this mean relative to our question, Why does personality change under stress?

Whether we consider stress as an internal state of the organism defined by antecedent conditions (stressors) and consequent behaviors (disruption) or whether we consider stress as a stimulus condition, the researcher must still ask the question about stress and personality in terms of systematic relationships between specific stimulus situations and specific changes in behavior. If stress is not defined as a "state of the organism" but as a stimulus situation, one need not draw inferences about the intervening processes between "stress and personality." We *may* draw them, and we often do (for example, loud noises may be claimed to produce *fear* that interferes with concentration and subsequently disrupts *learning*), but such an inferential process is not *necessary*. By defining stress as a stimulus situation, we avoid viewing the concept as the internal process that *mediates* or *causes* the observed disruptions in behavior.

For purposes of this book we have chosen to define stress as a stimulus situation rather than as an internal process or state. Thus, studies classified by the original investigators in various other ways than studies of stress (studies of fear, deprivation, and so on) fall directly under the umbrella of our general question.

What can psychologists do to help? It has been argued that all "basic research" may ultimately turn out to help in that knowledge will always, sooner or later, be applied in some way. Clearly, that is not what is meant by the question being analyzed. The intended meaning of the question is, What can psychologists do to help someone NOW? Much available research deals with this. Psychologists in industry try to prevent and reduce stress, or try to deal with reactions to stress. Their methods include complex, large-scale projects, such as modifying the work environment to make it less stressful, and also include attempts to measure people's capabilities and interests so that the right person may be placed on the right job. Some psychologists are trying to develop new methods of teaching and learning, hoping to alleviate the stress of failure in school, while still other psychologists are trying to develop techniques to help people reduce conflict. But the sort of psychologist one thinks of on hearing the word *help* is the "clinical psychologist" who tries to assist people who are unable to cope with the stress in their lives.

Clinical psychology is often referred to as "one of the helping professions." This means that much of what practicing clinical psychologists do involves working with people having difficulties in their lives. "Clinical services" vary widely, and the different activities involved cannot be easily summarized. As examples, however, you might find a clinical psychologist talking with the parents of a mentally retarded child in order to plan a long-term educational program. Another may be assisting a couple having problems in their marriage, while a third may be trying to help someone who has been threatening to commit suicide These and many other services are delivered to people in a number of settings including: mental hospitals, general hospitals, medical schools, universities, community mental health clinics, and private practice offices. But in terms of our question, it is necessary to be more explicit about what is meant by the term *help*.

In the context of this book, *help* means engaging in some specifiable action or set of actions designed to reduce, eliminate, or prevent responses to stress that are in some way undesirable.

The plan of the rest of the book. In Part II of this book we are first going to present some research studies that address questions about how animals and people react to stress. We will then present several studies that deal with what psychologists can do about it, that is, questions relating to how psychologists might help people. The investigations you will read in Part II have all been reported in various scientific publications, but they are not "readings" in that they are not word-for-word copies of the published reports. We have rewritten these studies in nontechnical language, or defined simply whatever technical terms we have used.

You will see in each section in Part II how the investigator has asked a question that we considered to be related to our grand question. Each study we report will start with a question that is considerably narrower but definitely, in some sense, a part of that grand question. You should look for some repeated themes in the various sections of Part II. For example, note that when concepts are defined in terms of observables, the question becomes even narrower. Such definitions allow objective observation and make it possible for other investigators to repeat the study, but may have the bad effect of taking the investigator far down the ladder of specificity and far away from the original question. Note also in the studies in Part II the careful attention to the concept of control. Recall that we distinguished between related meanings of the word *control*. We will show in each section just how observations were made in a controlled fashion and also how unwanted sources of potential influence were eliminated from the experiments.

Part III, as we have said, relies heavily on your having read carefully the studies of Part II. We will use the studies to talk about some general principles of psychological research, and we will raise some critical questions about psychological research in general, as it is represented for you by the studies you will read in Part II and in your course text. We urge you to read the investigations with all of the critical ability you can muster. We are going to raise, as we just noted, criticisms ourselves. The studies we picked are *good* studies. We did *not* select studies because they had flaws we could later attack. But science is a human enterprise. As such it has limitations.

Part II Some Questions, Some Answers

DOES CHILDHOOD STRESS AFFECT ADULT PERSONALITY?

or many years psychologists have been interested in the developmental aspect of the "grand question," What is the relationship between a person's experiences during childhood and that person's adult personality? This is such a broad question that it is impossible to provide a meaningful answer. The scientist must break this question down to manageable proportions. While one could begin by asking what is meant by *childhood* (that is, what age) and what is meant by *adult personality*, we can first ask, What experiences are we talking about? and What aspects of childhood are we interested in?

Years ago Sigmund Freud, a Viennese physician, formulated a theory of behavior centering about the importance of what he called childhood *trauma* or *stress*. One of his basic ideas was that adult personality is profoundly influenced by the traumatic or stressful experiences of childhood. Freud argued that as children develop, they all progress through the same series of stages, which he called "stages of psychosexual development." During the first stage, the oral stage, the infant is almost totally involved with activities concerning the mouth: sucking, eating, lip smacking, gurgling, and so forth. The second stage Freud termed the anal stage. In this stage, he argued, the infant is primarily concerned with activity centering around the anus: elimination, toilet training, smearing feces, and so forth. Freud hypothesized that the third, or phallic, stage finds the child interested in the manipulation of, and activities concerned with, the genitals. In the fourth, or latency, stage the child theoretically drops interest in bodily zones and becomes involved with school, peers, and so on. Ideally, the child develops through the stages into a mature, stable adult. This assumes that all goes pretty well during the stages. But, according to the theory, if stress interferes with the normal developmental process, then personality is affected, and the effects are carried into adulthood. Freud also theorized that the way that personality is affected depends on the stage of development in which the stress occurs and on the nature of the stress.

How does this brief theoretical outline fit into our scheme? We began with the grand and unanswerable question, How does childhood affect adult personality? We have fit the question into a theoretical context from which specific predictions can be made. We can now ask a question related to some specific aspect of childhood, for ex-

15

ample, What will happen to adult personality when stress is related to oral activity? This is still unanswerable. The definition of adult personality is lacking. Also we have not yet defined what is meant by trauma or stress, nor have we defined specifically what is meant by oral activity. What we have done is used a theory to narrow our grand question to a more specific realm of childhood experience. We have also identified in a general way the experience we want to study (that is, stress or trauma). So let's pursue this narrowing process even further. The major oral activity is eating. We can define another term in our question, If there is stress or trauma related to childhood eating experience, what is the effect on adult personality? The nature of the stress is still undefined, as is adult personality, but the question has been narrowed. Let us now attack the remaining ambiguities.

Clinicians and anthropologists have made observations over the years, which have led them to believe that adults who have experienced feeding frustration as infants are competitive and quarrelsome, and tend to hoard food. On the other hand, casual observations have suggested that when children are fed in loving ways and not frustrated, they become generous and cooperative adults. Given these observations, we can again narrow our question, making it less and less grand. We have begun to define what we mean by stress and by adult personality. We can now begin to formulate a crude, preliminary hypothesis: Stress in the form of feeding frustration during infancy will cause the adult to develop personality traits like competitiveness, hoarding, and uncooperativeness.

But how do we go about testing this notion in keeping with the scientific principles outlined previously? First of all, we must ask the general question, What kind of experimental design is needed to test the hypothesis? We could observe two groups of infants, one group whose feeding is accompanied by some relatively severe, frustrating experience, and another group whose feeding is accomplished with "tender, loving care." We would then have to wait for twenty or more years, and at that time make the observations necessary to determine whether or not the predicted differences would appear in the adult personalities of the two groups. If they did and if we were able to rule out other possible explanations, then we would have confirmed our hypothesis. We would have also lent some support to the theory. However, that last "if" is a big one.

It is practically impossible to make all of the observations necessary to rule out the possibility that some factor other than the frustration caused the difference. It is almost certain that mothers who feed their infants lovingly and those who feed them stressfully differ in many, many ways unrelated to feeding. They may tend to use different methods of discipline, express affection differently, and so on. Can that problem be resolved by establishing sufficient control over two groups of infants so that we could guarantee that their childhood experiences were highly similar except for differences in feeding? The answer to the latter question is No. Clearly, it would be profoundly unethical to deal with people this way.

So the obvious direct approach to this question of feeding frustration and adult personality is unworkable. What is the alternative? We could abandon the question. Or we could use subjects other than people, perhaps rats. The use of animals is clearly not optimal in terms of our original question because rats are obviously not humans. Nevertheless, with animals we could do the research and not have to be concerned with the ethical and methodological problems involved in studying children.

Assuming that we decide to approach our question using rats as subjects, we must define the terms in our question so that the relevant experimental manipulations and observations can be made. We must select manipulations defining stress in terms of feeding frustration, manipulations that can be made in a controlled fashion on rats. We must select indexes of personality that can be observed objectively and reliably in rats.

An actual study by J. McV. Hunt demonstrates how this is done. In 1941, Hunt began asking "grand" questions about childhood experiences and adult personality in much the same way as we began this section. He, too, came to the same conclusions regarding the need for using nonhuman subjects, and chose rats. Let us see how he went about defining the terms in the question and testing the hypothesis.

As we indicated above, one of the first things that had to be decided was, What is meant by infancy? On the basis of the rate of biological development of the species, and in light of his question, Hunt decided to focus on a period of time closely following weaning, which in rats occurs approximately twenty-one days after birth. Next it was necessary to define feeding frustration objectively. In the case of his experiment he allowed twenty-four-day-old animals to eat for only ten minutes at a time after being forced to go without food over varying lengths of time. This treatment lasted for fifteen days. Thus, two of the crucial elements have been defined: childhood and feeding frustration. The next thing to be decided was, What will be called adulthood? Again on the basis of developmental considerations, Hunt chose an age of approximately six months to represent the adult rat. Thus at the end of the six-month period he was ready to ask the question, What effect, if any, has the childhood experience of feeding frustration (the stress situation) had upon the adult personality? Still another problem of definition had to be resolved. Recall that earlier we referred to some anecdotal and clinical evidence suggesting that stress related to eating made people uncooperative, selfish, and so forth. Hunt had to reduce these statements to some aspect of rat behavior that he could measure.

He decided to measure *hoarding behavior*, the amount of food a nonhungry animal would carry back to its cage. This was quantified as the number of food pellets stored over a series of four trials lasting thirty minutes each, one trial per day for four days.

Let us summarize what has been said up to now. We started out with a grand question, What is the effect of childhood experience upon adult personality? Freud's theory, plus some unsystematic observations, helped us narrow the question to, What is the result of feeding frustration on adult personality? As we progressed, it became important, for many reasons, to finally reduce our grand question until it now can be stated as, What effect does depriving twenty-four-day-old rats of food over a fifteen-day period have on the storage of food pellets during a series of thirty-minute periods after the rats have matured to six months of age? The question is made even more specific in that the mature rats were frustrated prior to the hoarding tests by keeping them on a "subsistence diet" for five days. The question is not so grand anymore, but now we can answer it by making objective observations relevant to its now narrowed form. Let's continue.

One very important aspect of scientific research has not yet been included in our discussion of Hunt's research: that is, the concept of control—the experimental procedure to rule out as many explanations of the results as possible. Now that the question has been reduced to manageable size we must include in our experiment the controls necessary to obtain a scientifically meaningful answer.

Since Hunt intended to demonstrate that the stressful childhood experience, as he defined it, had an effect on adult personality, again as he defined it, he had to show that rats that had *not* received the childhood eating stress did *not* develop the hoarding behavior. Thus the question becomes one of comparing groups of rats, a frustrated group and a nonfrustrated group. In order to make the results of the comparisons more interpretable, Hunt did not just use any two groups of rats. He obtained genetically matched groups of rats by splitting litters in such a fashion that each rat in the experimental group had a genetically similar littermate in the control group.

But Hunt wished to go further. He also wanted to determine if the *particular age during infancy* at which feeding frustration occurred was an important determinant of adult hoarding behavior. In order to answer this aspect of the question, two more groups of rats were needed. One additional group had to undergo the feeding frustration *later* than twenty-four days in infancy. Hunt decided to use thirty-two-day-old rats. A second control group of matched thirty-two-day-old rats had to be given the normal eating experience. We might diagram the experimental design as follows:

Group	Type of infantile feeding experience	Measure of behavior in adulthood following five days of "subsistence" eating
Experimental Group I	Frustrated at 24 days of age	Number of pellets hoarded
Control Group I	Unlimited food	Number of pellets hoarded
Experimental Group II	Frustrated at 32 days of age	Number of pellets hoarded
Control Group II	Unlimited food	Number of pellets hoarded

Prior to initiating the hoarding test in adulthood, Hunt observed the rats' behavior during a time when they were allowed to eat freely. No differences in hoarding appeared among the groups.

Now there are two major comparisons to make in attempting to answer the question. The first is a comparison between the twenty-four-day-old frustration group and their control group, Control I. If, at the end of the six months, Experimental Group I hoards more pellets than Control Group I, then Hunt could say that feeding frustration does affect later behavior. If, in addition, Experimental Group II does not hoard more than Control Group II, then Hunt would have evidence not only that infantile feeding-frustration affects later behavior, but also that the time of such infantile frustration is crucial. If Experimental Group II does hoard more than their controls, this would provide further evidence that infantile frustration is important but would not support the contention that the specific time of such frustration is of any consequence. If the hoarding was found in the twenty-four-day-old frustration group (Experimental Group I) and not in the thirty-two-day-old frustration group (Experimental Group II) Hunt could argue that not only is it feeding frustration in infancy but feeding frustration early in infancy that is important in determining adult hoarding behavior.

So the experiment demands four groups of rats—all necessary to answer our not very grand, but answerable, question, What did Hunt find, and how do his answers relate to the grand question?

First of all, the twenty-four-day-old frustration group (Experimental Group I) hoarded more in later life than did Control Group I. Experimental Group II did not differ in hoarding behavior from Control Group II. In fact, the latter three groups did not differ from one another with respect to hoarding, but they all hoarded less than the twenty-four-day-old group.

Can we now say that childhood feeding frustration leads to adult hoarding behavior? No. What we can say is that, given the specific operations used in Hunt's experiment, stressing twenty-four-day-old rats by feeding frustration produced hoarding at six months of age while the same manipulation on thirty-two-day-old rats did not effectively produce adult hoarding. Can we say anything about human behavior? Not directly. We can't even say much about childhood or adulthood, since it is very difficult to talk in these terms when we are dealing with rats. But there is one point that we cannot forget: While the grand question has not been answered, we have more information related to it than we had before. We now know that certain kinds of stress will affect certain kinds of later behavior at least in one species. The findings are highly consistent with certain theories regarding the effects of early experience on later behavior. They *lend support* to the theories with which they are consistent. Continued research with a variety of manipulations of stress and a variety of measures of personality in a variety of species will perhaps lead us closer to an understanding of the relationships involved. Perhaps an understanding of the laws relating early stress experience to adult behavior in infrahuman species will enable us to look at human behavior in a new light and to understand it more thoroughly. In other words, perhaps seeing the relevant factors in the relatively controllable experiments with infrahuman organisms will tell us what to look for in the less controllable studies of human behavior.

One final comment on the Hunt study should be made. While the hypothesis was confirmed and the theory from which it was deduced was thereby supported, the theory was in no sense *proven*. Any number of other theoretical positions besides Freudian psychoanalysis postulate long-term effects of disadvantageous early experience. In addition to the alternative-theory problem, Hunt's study is but one study—with one manipulation of stress and one measure of personality in one species.

CAN STRESS CAUSE ULCERS?

The term *executive* calls up many images: big office, big desk, big car, and big problems to handle. In a psychology-conscious America, it also calls up the image of that person as distressed, driven, ulcer-ridden by the recurrent pressure to make decisions affecting not only a single life but the lives of others as well. To the extent that this image is correct, it reflects an insight into a relationship between stress and one of the most fundamental characteristics of personality—emotional behavior. Our everyday language vividly depicts the emotional reactions of a person under stress with such phrases as, "She's eating her insides out," or "Something is gnawing at him." It seems, in short, that people today commonly recognize that psychological stress can have far-reaching effects physiologically as well as psychologically. But just how well understood is the relationship between stress and person-ality—between stress and the behaviors that produce physiological damage such as ulcers?

Some fascinating scientific attempts have been made to uncover the key elements in the development of ulcer-producing emotional be-havior under conditions of stress. One of the attempts is the research carried on by Joseph V. Brady and others at the Walter Reed Army Institute of Research (Brady, 1958). Brady and his colleagues began this program with a somewhat different interest. They had spent several years studying the more general problem of the relation between stress and emotionality before some surprising results led them to concen-trate on the relationship between stress and ulceration. In their emo-tionality research they had settled on monkeys as subjects because monkeys can ". . . be studied under controlled conditions, and it is through animal experiments that we are finding leads to the cause of ulcers as well as to the effect of emotional stress on the organism in general" (Brady, 1958, p. 96).

The kind of manipulation that Brady and his colleagues used was placing an animal in a restraining chair and then having the animal learn to press a lever frequently to avoid electric shocks. The monkeys were taught to press the lever by a procedure called operant condition-ing. In this case the reinforcement (that is, the payoff) for learning and making the response was the avoidance of the shock.

The restraining chair made sure that the monkey was where the experimenter wanted it when he wanted it. The monkey could not run away and escape the electric shock. The restraining chair was serving as a control factor, preventing extraneous stimuli that might influence other responses of the animal from entering into the experiment. This is important, since the experimenters were interested in observing the effects of their conditioning procedures on emotional responses. This particular control introduced by the experimenters, however, in it-self seemed to be introducing unwanted influences into the research. The physical restraint imposed upon these energetic monkeys itself elicited emotional responses. It was a stress situation. The investigators decided to take some physiological measures to get some information about the internal biological effects of the chair and conditioning procedures. A preliminary study showed that the stress situation did, in fact, radically change the level of certain hormones in the animals' blood. This finding encouraged the researchers to do a large-scale study with nineteen monkeys. In a short time, the surprising results brought the research to a halt. Many of the monkeys died!

Postmortem examinations revealed that many of the monkeys had developed massive stomach ulcers, which are relatively rare in laboratory monkeys. As an influential American psychologist, B. F. Skinner, has put it, "When you run onto something interesting, drop everything else and study it" (Skinner, 1959, p. 363). Brady and his colleagues did just that and promptly shifted the focus of their research to factors producing ulceration. They were convinced from extensive prior research that it could not be the influence of the chair alone, but they had to design an experiment that would somehow control the effect of the restraining chair. The conditioning procedure that they were using seemed to be the primary stress, the cause of the fatal ulcers. However, this procedure is complex, and the effect on the animals could have been due to any one of several aspects of the situation or perhaps to the effect of several of them acting together.

Brady and his colleagues controlled for many of the unwanted sources of potential influences with a very ingenious experimental setup. They continued using the restraining chair, but each experimental animal was paired with a control animal that was held in a restraining chair in exactly the same way and for exactly the same period of time as the experimental animal. Furthermore, each time the experimental animal failed to press the lever and thus got a shock, the *control animal also got a shock* of precisely the same duration and precisely the same intensity. The control animal also had a lever, identical with that in the experimental animal's chamber, but one that could not prevent shock. Consider for a moment what the experimenters have accomplished with this *yoked-control* procedure. The two monkeys are in virtually identical environments, same restraint, same visual surroundings, same sounds—same everything *except* for the condition that the experimenters suspected was crucial. That condition was the stress involved in the requirement to constantly press the lever to avoid shock, that is, to "make decisions."

The details of the experimental procedure are important. The "executive monkey" was required to press the lever at least once every twenty seconds in order to avoid a 5-milliampere, 60-cycle, .5-second electrical shock. The monkey was required to "work" on a six-hour-on, six-hour-off schedule. No shocks at all were delivered during the "off" periods, with these periods being identified for the animals by the presence of a red light.

What happened?   The executive monkey learned its task well. The subject averaged between fifteen and twenty lever presses per minute and didn't even slow down, until it died! After twenty-three days of the conditioning procedures, the executive suddenly died of a massive perforated ulcer. The control monkey, who had been equally restrained and equally shocked, was healthy. A second pair of animals was subjected to the same conditioning procedure and again the executive monkey died of ulcers—this time after twenty-five days. A third executive lasted but nine days, and a fourth, forty-eight. Autopsies on all four of the executive monkeys revealed massive ulcers, while autopsies on the controls revealed none. The ulcers were truly psychosomatic; that is, actual physical damage resulted from stress that was essentially psychological.

The research team continued their experimentation on the nature of the relationships involved. Possibly, social factors might have been important, since the executive and control could and did communicate with each other. The researchers, therefore, studied several more pairs of monkeys, keeping all the contingencies the same as before, save one. This time they isolated the two members of a pair from one another. The executives still developed ulcers and died; the controls did not.

In an effort to vary the level of stress and observe the effects on ulceration, the researchers tried schedules of shock-on and shock-off periods other than six hours on, six hours off. They expected that an eighteen on, six off (eighteen hours of decisions and six hours of rest) regime would speed up the ulceration—but it did not. The experimenters were surprised to find that none of these monkeys developed ulcers. They tried thirty minutes on—thirty minutes off, with shocks *every two seconds!* The executives worked at their bar pressing frantically for weeks—but again none of them developed ulcers! No other schedule of work and rest periods (perhaps it would be more appropriate to say stress and rest periods) caused stomach ulcers.

The results showed clearly that the emotional stress, in order to produce ulceration, had to be intermittent, and since not all intermittent schedules "worked," the stress cycles apparently coincided with some natural biological cycle of the organism. In order to get a clearer picture of what was happening, the experimenters analyzed the acidity of some of the monkeys' stomachs over the duration of the experiment. Again they came up with some surprising findings. Stomach acidity remained fairly low and constant during stress but rose sharply during the rest period! The sharpest rise occurred during rest periods following six-hour stress periods, while there was none at all following a one-hour stress session. This surely describes one link of what must be a long chain of events that intervene between psychological stress and the production of ulcers and *may* be relevant to an understanding of the stressful conditions that lead to ulcers in people.

Brady and his colleagues have by no means fully described the relationship between stress and ulceration, much less the relationship between stress and personality. Brady himself takes pains to point out that there is a great deal that they do *not* know. For example, what other kinds of stress might have the same effects? What other effects did their procedures generate that they might have failed to measure, simply because they were not looking for them? There are many such questions, and, if the reader does not mind even more repetition, each of these would have to be broken down into answerable questions!

Unlike Hunt, Brady and his co-workers were not attempting to test an aspect of a comprehensive theory. Like Hunt, they began by asking an important question but answered highly specific ones instead.

DOES MISERY LOVE COMPANY?

 e began our discussion by asking a question that was worded in an unanswerable form, Why does one's personality change under stress? We have seen how two researchers have attempted to answer this question by breaking it down into smaller, more manageable parts. In our discussion up to now these parts have required the use of animals as experimental subjects. Let us now look at some research that attacks part of the problem, using human subjects—women students at the University of Minnesota.

Stanley Schachter is a psychologist who has been interested in questions of how and why people relate to one another. More specifically, he has been interested in why some people want to be around other people a great deal of the time, while others have less need to be in groups. Thus, in general, Schachter has been interested in the psychology of *affiliation*. Let's see how this interest has led him to study the relationship between stress and personality, and how his experimental problem developed (Schachter, 1959).

Much speculation and anecdotal evidence has suggested that social isolation produces anxiety, or, in other words, is stressful. Because of "intuitive reasons," as Schachter put it, it seemed reasonable to expect that stress-producing situations would lead to an increase in "affiliative tendencies." Putting this into our framework, Schachter began to ask the question, How does stress affect one aspect of personality, the desire to be with others? Clearly, this is an unanswerable question as stated. The operations needed to carry out a scientific study of the question are unspecified. As yet, we don't know how stress is defined, and we are even less clear concerning what is meant by "desire to be with others."

Schachter chose to define stress in terms of a situation in which the subjects (female college students) were led to anticipate painful stimulation. The experimental operations he used were relatively simple. He ushered the young women into a room full of electrical equipment, and he had a confederate tell them they were going to participate in an experiment on the effects of electric shock. This confederate also discussed things such as electroshock therapy, electrocution, and so forth. He then told the subjects that they were to receive painful shocks so that the effects could be studied scientifically. The exact instructions were as follows:

Allow me to introduce myself. I am Dr. Gregor Zilstein of the Medical School's Departments of Neurology and Psychiatry. I have asked you all to come today in order to serve as subjects in an experiment concerned with the effects of electrical shock.

(Zilstein paused ominously, then continued with a seven- or eight-minute recital of the importance of research in this area, citing electroshock therapy, the increasing number of accidents due to electricity, and so on. He concluded in this vein:)

What we will ask each of you to do is very simple. We would like to give each of you a series of electric shocks. Now, I feel I must be completely honest with you and tell you exactly what you are in for. These shocks will hurt, they will be painful. As you can guess, if, in research of this sort, we're to learn anything at all that will really help humanity, it is necessary that our shocks be intense. What we will do is put an electrode in your hand, hook you into apparatus such as this (Zilstein points to the electrical-looking gadgetry behind him), give you a series of electric shocks, and take various measures such as your pulse rate, blood pressure, and so on. Again, I do want to be honest with you and tell you that these shocks will be quite painful but, of course, they will do no permanent damage. (Schachter, 1959, p. 13)

Thus the situation was designed to include a specific set of operations that most observers would agree would constitute stress. Now it was necessary to develop an objective definition of the aspect of personality to be studied, the desire to be with others, or affiliation. In order to explain how this was defined, we will outline the experiment. Remember that the question is, How does stress affect the desire to be with others? What type of experimental design is necessary to answer the question? Clearly, we need subjects who are in a stressful situation, but how will we be able to evaluate their behavior unless we have some behavior to compare it with? We need a group of subjects that is not stressed. Thus we have the beginnings of an experimental design. Stressed versus nonstressed subjects are to be compared in terms of which group indicates more of a desire to be with others. How is this handled in terms of operations? We have already seen how stress was defined. But what about the nonstressed group? The women were brought into the same room minus the electrical equipment. Essentially they were told that they were to participate in a study of the effects of electric shock, but that there would be no pain involved and nothing to fear. This operation defines the nonstressed group. The exact instructions were:

I have asked you all to come today in order to serve as subjects in an experiment concerned with the effects of electric shock. I hasten to add, do not let the word "shock" trouble you; I am sure that you will enjoy the experiment. (Then precisely the same recital on the importance of the research, concluding with:)

What we will ask each one of you to do is very simple. We would like to give each of you a series of very mild electric shocks. I assure you that what you will feel will not in any way be painful. It will resemble more a tickle or a tingle than anything unpleasant. We will put an electrode on your hand, give you a series of very mild shocks and measure such things as your pulse rate and blood pressure, measures with which I'm sure you are all familiar from visits to your family doctor. (Schachter, 1959, p. 13)

We still need to define affiliation objectively. How was this handled? Once the experimental manipulations were completed, all subjects were told that there would be a ten-minute delay while the equipment was set up. During this period, they were told that they could wait in some other rooms, which were very comfortable. The essential part of these instructions, however, was telling the subjects that they could either wait alone or wait with other subjects who were also participants in the experiment. They were then given a questionnaire with five choices:

1. I very much prefer being alone.
2. I prefer being alone.
3. I don't care very much.
4. I prefer being together with others.
5. I very much prefer being together with others.

Each subject was asked to indicate her preference, and it was the response to this questionnaire that defined affiliation. Note the objectivity of the measure. Schachter did not say that "the young women seemed to want company." He could point to a check mark on a scale—behavior that any competent observer would agree on. A 5 is a 5, no matter who looks at it. The subjects were never shocked. Once they answered the questionnaire, the experiment was completed, and Schachter explained the whole procedure to all subjects so that they understood what he had done and why.

Before looking at Schachter's findings, let us summarize what we have seen so far. We began with the grand and unanswerable question, Why does one's personality change under stress? We saw that Schachter was interested in one aspect of personality, affiliation, and that he asked the narrower question, How does stress affect the need to affiliate with others? He then reduced his question so that it became, How does telling people they are going to be painfully shocked affect their response to a series of questions relating to affiliation as compared to the effect of telling people they will be shocked but experience no pain?

What were the results? Schachter used a total of sixty-two subjects, thirty-two in the stress group and thirty in the no-stress group. Twenty stressed subjects elected to "be together"; nine indicated they didn't care while only three chose to be alone. Of the no-stress subjects ten wished to be together, eighteen didn't care, and two wished to be alone. These findings clearly suggest that stress increased the tendency to be with others as measured by the questionnaire. But Schachter was not satisfied with this answer. He argued that even though it seems that stress produced the desire to affiliate, the experiment did not tell us *why* stress produced that desire. In fact, he pointed out that there may be a number of reasons for his results. For example, it is possible that the choice to be with others represents a desire to be with *certain* people, people who are in the same miserable situation. The previous experiment provides no evidence with respect to this possible interpretation. Schachter wanted to determine whether stress produces a generalized need to affiliate or a specific need to be with others in the same plight. This latter explanation is a kind of misery-loves-company interpretation.

So the first experiment has suggested a second. The new question is, Given that stress produces a desire to be with others, can these others be just anybody, or are they people who are undergoing the same stress? Clearly if Schachter wants to interpret the findings of the first experiment in light of this second question, he should use operational definitions similar to those in the first experiment and change only what is necessary to answer the second question. Let's see what he did. First of all, the question requires only stressed subjects. We already know from the first experiment that stress, as defined, produces affiliative tendencies, as measured. So Schachter used exactly the same instructions in the second experiment. But *all* of the subjects were told that the shock would be painful. There was one difference, however. In the first experiment the subjects were in groups when they received the instructions. In the second experiment they were introduced to the procedure individually. This was necessary in order to make it possible to interpret the results clearly. The study would have been confounded if the subjects had known each other, since a choice to affiliate might mean that the subjects wanted to be with people they knew rather than with others in the same "misery."

Once the subjects had undergone the instructions, it was necessary to do something that would allow Schachter to measure their affiliative preferences. Therefore, he again changed the procedure from the first experiment. As before, all subjects were told that they had to wait for ten minutes. This time, however, some were told they could either wait alone or with other young women waiting to talk with their advisors. The rest of the subjects were told they could wait alone or with other subjects also taking part in the same experiment. Again, the measure of affiliation was a questionnaire, very similar to the one above.

Once the experiment was completed, the whole thing was explained to the participants. Now let us see what the results were. The young women who had the choice of being alone or with others participating in the experiment chose to be with the group significantly more often than did those who had the choice of being alone or with those waiting to see their advisors. Thus Schachter was able to refine further the answer to his initial research question. He could now state: Given the conditions of the previous experiment, stressed people tend to affiliate with others who are under the same stress. This sounds like a fine and direct answer, and indeed it is. But this is not the end. Many other questions are still unanswered, even within the framework of this somewhat limited question on stress and affiliation. For example, would the same results occur if male rather than female subjects were used? Is the affiliation-stress relationship discovered here limited to college students who are, for the most part, middle-class, white Protestants? Schachter was able to shed some light on the question of the specificity of affiliation within the context of his experimental conditions. A question that still must be answered is, How specific must the stress situation be? That is, will any stress also make them want to seek out the company of others, or must the stress be of a certain type? We could raise many interesting and important questions suggested by this research, but the point is that these two studies have attacked only a very small part of the already fragmented grand question. They are interesting and well-done experiments. They provide a bit of information we did not have before. We know a little more about personality and stress. But as the reader can see from the few questions stated above, there is not yet a complete answer to the question of how stress and affiliation are related. A more complete answer will come only after much more research, and even then it will not be an answer to the grand question, How does stress affect personality?

CAN LEARNING CREATE STRESS SITUATIONS?

e have seen that there are a number of ways that the question—Why does one's personality change when under stress?—can be approached. The wording of the question seems to imply that what is stressful for one person is stressful for another. Our analysis of the concept of stress certainly implies that this is the case, but the situation is not so simple. Some people react negatively to situations that most others find neutral or even pleasant! In other words, many situations that would *not* be generally identified as constituting stress produce very disruptive responses in some people.

The "big question" raised by these differences is, Why do some situations constitute stress for some people and not for others? One possible but very general answer to this question is learning. That is, people *learn* various ways to respond to situations in the environment. Under certain circumstances the responses they learn may be very disruptive and maladaptive ones.

We are dealing here with a fundamental issue in psychology, that of individual differences. While individual differences can arise from biological sources, psychologists have suggested that some significant differences among people are learned differences. How does this apply to our questions regarding stress? We could ask, *How* do people learn to respond to certain situations as stress? This question assumes that individual differences in what *constitutes* stress *can be learned*. The question of *how* people learn is a question about the learning process itself. Perhaps the first question to answer would be, *Can* people learn to respond to situations or stimuli as stress? This is the question that Neal Miller (1948) addressed.

Up to the time of Miller's experiment it was a well-established fact that animals and humans will learn habits, or responses, to escape from stress such as pain, heat, or shock. But Miller wanted to know what would happen when a situation that had not been stressful before was associated with pain. Would an animal learn a *new* response to escape it? That would show that the situation had become a stress situation as a function of learning. Let us see how Miller investigated this. The terms of the question as stated so far are much too general. As in all of our other research examples, words like stress and learn must be reduced to operations. To see how this was accomplished, we can begin by describing the apparatus used in the experiment.

A 36 × 6 × 8½-inch box was built and divided into two 18-inch compartments. One of these compartments was painted white and had a floor made of metal rods that could be electrified. The second compartment was painted black and had a solid, nonelectrifiable floor. The two compartments were separated by a door that could be opened either by the subject turning a wheel or pressing a bar inside the box or by the experimenter pressing a button. The experimenter determined the method that opened the door.

In this experiment the neutral stimulus was the white compartment *before* the grid floors were electrified. In the present context, neutral means, as we shall see, that subjects showed no preference for either the white or the black compartment prior to experiencing shock. This stimulus was, of course, made up of all of the cues available in the compartment including color, shape, and feel of the bars on the animals' feet. The stress was represented by electric shock. Miller hoped to show that rats would learn to escape the white part of the box after being shocked there. Escape from the compartment would be taken as evidence that this portion of the apparatus had become stress. There was a series of steps that had to be accomplished in order to establish this relationship.

First, it was necessary to show that the white box was, in fact, a neutral stimulus (not yet stress). Next it was necessary to associate this neutral stimulus with the known stress (shock) so that animals would have the opportunity to learn to escape from it. The third step was to find out if the white compartment really had become a stress stimulus (did the learning really occur?). If these three steps could be accomplished, one could argue that a neutral or nonstressful situation can, through learning, become a stress stimulus. However, Miller did not wish to stop there. He asked a fourth question. As we have said, it was well known that organisms could learn to escape from painful situations. However, an interesting and important question was, Can such a learned stress stimulus produce new learning when painful shocks are no longer presented in the situation? In terms of the present experiment, once the white compartment becomes stressful, can it motivate the learning of a *new* escape response? Now what were the operations used in these four steps?

Miller decided to use twenty-five rats as subjects. His first step, aimed at demonstrating that the white compartment was not a stressful stimulus, was to put each subject into the box for one minute with the door between compartments open. He then observed and recorded the animals' behavior. In no case did the rats show any tendency either to stay in *or* to avoid either of the two compartments. Thus Miller assumed that being in the white compartment was a neutral (or nonstressful) situation for the rat. Clearly, being in the white compartment is no more stressful than being in the black, at least, when stress is objectively defined and measured in terms of preference behavior. If subjects had tended to avoid the white compartment, then it would not have been possible to assume neutrality, and another operation would have been used to measure the absence of stress.

The experimenter next placed each subject in the white compartment for ten trials with shock. Briefly, these trials involved putting the subjects in the compartment, turning on shock (or in later trials putting animals in with shock already on), and opening the door for them with the experimenter's button. As you would expect, all of the animals ran rapidly through the door into the black compartment. But, has the white compartment itself become stressful? That is, will rats now escape from the white compartment when no shock is administered? To answer this question, Miller next placed the subjects into the white compartment with *no shock on*, and for five trials he observed that *all* animals continued to run rapidly through the opened door. Compare this behavior to the behavior observed in the apparatus prior to the shock trials. The animals' behavior has changed! Where before they had shown *no* tendency to avoid or escape the white compartment, they now escaped rapidly from it even though no shock was present. The white compartment is clearly no longer neutral. It has become a stress stimulus. Note, however, that these general terms have, in reality, been reduced considerably to specific operations. Neutrality was demonstrated by showing that the subjects had no preference for one compartment or the other. The presence of stress was first defined in terms of running from one compartment to the other during shock. Now we are saying that the white compartment itself is a stress stimulus—that is, it produced escape responding just as did shock. Learning has taken place because a change in the behavior of the rats occurred as a function of their experience.

The next question is, Can this new, learned stress motivate the learning of a different escape response? In other words, can this now nonneutral situation have the same effect as a known stress, that is, shock? Will rats acquire some new response to escape it? Not only is this an interesting question in and of itself, but it is an important question in terms of making sense out of the experiment so far. One could argue that the white compartment really has not become a stress stimulus at all. An argument could be made that the animals escaped in the five nonshock trials because they learned a running habit in response to shock and that this habit simply persisted through the few nonshock trials. You can reject this argument if the subjects were able to learn a totally new response to get away from the white compartment. Did they?

Miller modified the apparatus so that turning the wheel in the white compartment would open the door. Then he put the rats in the white compartment with no shock and with the door closed. They were kept there for one hundred seconds per trial unless they turned the wheel and escaped. All subjects received sixteen such trials and the time it took them to open the door was recorded.

Thirteen of the twenty-five animals learned to turn the wheel and escape the white compartment. For eleven of these thirteen, the amount of time that they spent in the compartment on each trial before turning the wheel decreased sharply as trials progressed. In other words, learning was occurring for over one-half of the subjects with the only apparent stress being the previously neutral white compartment. This compartment not only had become a stress stimulus but also functioned in a way similar to the shock—it provided the basis for the learning of a totally new response. Escape learning is objectively defined here by the fact that subjects opened the door and by the fact that their performance over trials, measured by speed of responding, improved.

But Miller was not through. He asked yet another question, What if wheel-turning was no longer an effective response? What if turning the wheel no longer opened the door and led to escape? Would the animals learn yet *another* escape response? To explore this question, the thirteen rats that had learned to wheel-turn were put back into the white compartment. However, this time the wheel would not open the door. The animals had to press a bar (the new response to be learned) to escape into the black side of the box. Within ten trials, all thirteen subjects were pressing the bar to escape. Twelve of these animals improved over trials; that is, the time it took them to make the response once they were placed in the apparatus got shorter and shorter. Again learning was occurring! Miller points out that at first animals did wheel-turn, but this ineffective response was soon abandoned in favor of bar pressing. So it was demonstrated that the previously neutral compartment had become something more than a momentary stress. It had become powerful enough to motivate the learning of a wheel-turning response and powerful enough to motivate the abandoning of that response in favor of yet another response, bar pressing.

What has all this told us about our grand question, Why does personality change under stress? How did we get what may seem to be so far afield? Let's review what has happened. We have argued that in order to understand the relationships between stress and personality it would be important to know how some particular situations become stressful for one person and not for another. The answer was that the individual differences may be due to the different learning experiences that people have encountered.

Of course this is a very general and scientifically unsatisfactory answer. Multitudes of experiments are suggested, however, by the basic proposition. One small but important question raised is, Can a situation become a stress stimulus via a learning experience? If this question can be reduced to operations and answered experimentally, then we have added one bit of information that sheds light on our grand, general question.

We can say that Miller was able to show, at least within the limits of his experiment, that learning may account for the fact that some situations can constitute stress for some organisms and not for others. Also, he was able to show that this learning can provide the basis for acquiring additional responses. Furthermore, he has demonstrated that rats can *change* responses to stress as a function of learning. In fact, Miller's theoretical reason for doing the experiment was to see if animals could learn to "fear" previously neutral stimuli and to see if this "learned fear" would motivate the acquisition of new behaviors. Whether or not one wishes to infer the presence of fear as an internal state of the organism accompanying or provoked by the stress situation is unimportant for our purposes.

All of these broad interpretations or answers appear to be consistent with the data. But we must be careful in generalizing from the findings. Strictly speaking, Miller's research tells us that given certain organisms (rats of a particular age and strain), certain situations (his experimental apparatus), and certain stress (shock), particular responses (running escape, wheel turning, bar pressing) can be acquired in a given number of trials. Beyond this, we must use great caution in our interpretations of the experiment. As with other research, questions like, How general are Miller's findings? must be considered. The question of generalizability of research results will be discussed at length in Part III. It would be an error to take the findings too lightly. The results are important. From the standpoint of understanding complex human responses to stress, a small, but well-defined, bit of evidence has been obtained that may move us closer to answers related to the "grand question."

If you recall, we said in the very beginning of this book that the study of human behavior is so complex that "in actual practice a psychologist studies intensively some small aspect of one of the so-called simpler behavioral phenomena . . . to understand some small piece of the environment-organism interaction."

DOES TV VIOLENCE LEAD TO AGGRESSION UNDER STRESS?

I n the previous section we were concerned with the question of whether people might learn to fear previously neutral situations. That's an important part of the question about the relationship between stress and personality. Another question about the way in which learning fits into the picture is, How do different people learn to make different responses when they are in a given stress situation? Some run. Some freeze. Some fight. In this section we are interested in the ones who *fight*.

There are many possible explanations of why some people act aggressively under stress and some don't. One popular explanation is in terms of imitation. If we watch someone behave a certain way in a particular situation, we may behave the same way when we find ourselves in a similar situation. This is especially true if we saw that person getting rewarded for that behavior. A psychological theory, called social learning theory (Bandura, 1969), makes this argument.

Not all aggression is due to such a learning process, and not all aggression is in response to stress. But it seems reasonable that *some* aggression is triggered by stress. Fighting is one of the responses some people make under stress. One partial answer to the question of why this happens may be that some people learn to respond to stress with aggressive behavior by watching violence on TV. They learn that aggression under stress pays off, and this puts aggressive responses high on the "list" of behaviors to engage in when things get tough.

How can we get the data? Certainly the theory implies a cause-effect relation. We could do a laboratory experiment investigating the question. In fact, many have been done. Children have been exposed to violence on TV, and then their aggressive behavior toward other children has been measured (for example, Liebert & Baron, 1972). There are limitations on what we can infer from laboratory studies, which we will discuss in Part III. How else might we study the problem? We could go out into the "real world" and see if people who watch a great deal of violence on TV are really more aggressive than people who watch less TV violence.

One way psychologists answer questions about behavior is to read other people's research. Often, research done on one question is directly relevant to other questions. In this section we will call upon evidence that was produced by investigators who were not directly interested in the question, Why does one's personality change under stress? Nor were they directly concerned with how psychologists can help. They were interested in whether or not a causal relationship exists between preference for violent programs in childhood and aggressive behavior in adolescence. However, their results are interesting to someone studying stress and personality.

In 1960, several investigators (Eron, Walder, & Lefkowitz, 1971; Eron, Heusmann, Lefkowitz, & Walder, 1972) performed a large-scale investigation into the learning of aggression. They interviewed and obtained psychological test data on *every* third-grade child in Columbia County, New York—a total of 875 children. They interviewed at least one parent of most of these children. They interviewed teachers, and they obtained ratings of each child by other children.

Almost accidentally, they had found a relationship between television watching and aggressiveness. In the words of Eron, Walder, and Lefkowitz (1971),

A number of questions were inserted into the childrearing interview with parents to make it sound plausible to the respondent and to gain his cooperation. In a common-sense way, the relation to aggressive behavior of many questions that we asked must have seemed remote to the parents. Therefore randomly interspersed throughout the interview were items having to do with such matters as attendance at PTA meetings, TV habits of the children, comic books, and Spock's manual on childrearing (1957). These items were subsumed under one classification, facetiously called "Ladies Home Journal." The computer, unaware of our jokes, analyzed these responses along with the others. It was found that the number of hours children watched TV per week and the violence rating of their three favorite TV programs were both highly related to aggression as rated by peers (Eron, 1963). There was a significant positive relation between the violence ratings of children's favorite programs and aggressive behavior in school, although the relation between total number of hours watched and aggressive behavior was significantly negative. These findings, relating TV viewing habits and aggressive behavior in real life, corroborate the results obtained in the carefully controlled, and thus necessarily artificial, laboratory experiments of Bandura and his associates. . . . (pp. 39–40)

But then in 1970 they came back to Columbia County and set out to find whether the relationship between preference for violence on TV and aggressiveness was still there. They wanted to determine specifically whether preference for violence on TV in childhood was related to aggression in late adolescence. They went further than just looking for a relationship. They performed statistical analyses to see if their data supported the hypothesis that TV violence *causes* aggression.

The investigators stated their hypothesis as " . . . a young adult's aggressiveness is positively related to his preference for violent television when he was 8–9 years old and furthermore, that his preference for violent television during this critical period is one cause of his aggressiveness" (Eron et al., 1972, p. 253). "Young adult" meant about nineteen years old. The young adults were the same children who had been in the third grade in 1960, now ten years older. Of 875 children who had been studied in the third grade, 427 of these were located and living in the same community ten years later. Thus, the data of the study in 1970 was based upon two sets of measurements on 427 people—211 males and 216 females—measured ten years apart. The data in both investigations were composed mainly of interviews, ratings, and tests. The data are *observations*. Nothing was manipulated. Let's examine the measurement operations.

1960 measurements. Preference for violence on television was measured when the subjects were in the third grade—that is, at approximately nine years of age. There are two measurement problems in this statement. One is the definition of a violent program. The other is determining which programs the child preferred. The measurement operations were as follows. Each child's mother was asked to list her child's three favorite TV programs. No judgments of good or bad, violent or nonviolent were asked for or made. They just asked for names of programs. A list of all named programs was compiled and given to two raters. The raters categorized the programs as violent or nonviolent. They agreed on 94 percent of their ratings. The remaining 6 percent were discussed and disagreements resolved. These categories were used in assigning to each child a score on "preference for violence on TV," each child being assigned a score ranging from 0 to 3. If none of the three favorite programs had been rated as violent, that child's score was 0. If all three had been so rated, the score was 3.

Many other measures were taken on these children as well. These included socioeconomic factors, childrearing information, parental personality factors, IQ, and others. The most important additional measure was a rating of aggressiveness. This was done by using a "guess who" technique with the child's classmates. The children were given a list with the names of all of their classmates and were instructed to mark the names of all the children who fitted each of twenty-two questions as they were read aloud. Most of the twenty-two questions are listed below.

Who are you?
Who are the children who always sit around you?
Who would you like to sit next to in class?
*Who does not obey the teacher?
*Who often says, "Give me that"? (asked with emphasis)
*Who gives dirty looks or sticks out their tongues at other children?
Who is too busy to talk to other children?
*Who makes up stories and lies to get other children into trouble?
*Who does things that bother others?
*Who starts a fight over nothing?
*Who pushes or shoves children?
*Who is always getting into trouble?
*Who says mean things?
Who is always in and out of things?
*Who takes other children's things without asking?
Who says, "Excuse me," even when they have not done anything bad?

Who are the children you would like to have for your best friends? (Eron et al., 1971, p. 33)

The ten critical questions for our purposes are those dealing with aggression. These are marked with an asterisk. The measure of rated aggressiveness for a particular child was the number of times that child was named in answer to the critical items.

1970 measurements. With minor modifications, the same two key measures were taken on all of the youths who could be located in 1970. Since many of them were now out of school, acquaintances of the same age in the community filled out a modified "guess who" questionnaire.

Now the four critical measures have been described. They are preference for television violence in grade 3 (TVVL 3) and in "grade 13" (TVVL 13), and rated aggressiveness in grades 3 (AGG 3) and "13" (AGG 13). What were the results?

The data were analyzed separately for males and females because the average aggression scores for males was much higher than the average for females. The essential analyses provided measures of how strongly TV violence was related to aggression for boys and how strongly TV violence was related to aggression for girls. We are interested in measuring relative *strengths* of relationship. No one would claim that there is any one-to-one or perfect relationship between these factors being studied. Aggression is far too complex. *Many* factors influence aggressiveness. TV violence *may* be one, but if so, it is only one of many. So we need a method of analysis that is sensitive to imperfect, or partial relationships. The statistical method of doing this is called *correlation*. Correlation is a statistical term, but it is also a common-sense term. If you think of it as co-relation, you will be on the right track. A positive correlation in this context between, for example, TVVL 3 and AGG 3 would simply mean that children who preferred violent programs tended to be rated as highly aggressive, while children who preferred nonviolent programs tended to be rated as nonaggressive. Instead of presenting the actual numbers, we will report the correlational analyses in words, indicating by YES or NO whether there was statistical evidence of a relationship. Keep in mind that the relationships we report below as YES were at best moderate in strength of association.

Since the time at which the measures were taken is critical, we will present the data in terms of diagrams that show the time dimension clearly. The first diagram shows the relationship for boys.

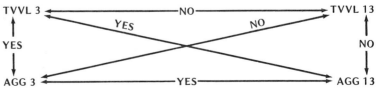

The second one shows the relationships for girls.

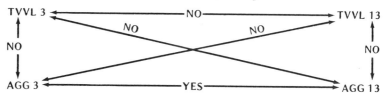

Only one relationship was significant in the girls' data; nine-year-old girls who were rated as aggressive were still rated as aggressive as young women. There is no evidence of any relationship between aggressiveness and TV preference. For the boys, a radically different pattern emerges. There is that same tendency for consistency from grades 3 to 13 in rated aggressiveness as there was for girls. However, the boys' data showed an association between preference for violence on TV in the third grade and rated aggressiveness in the third grade. That correlation is interesting. But the boys' data also showed the presence of the critical correlation—television violence in grade 3 and rated aggressiveness later in life. The association was not a strong one, but it was there!

In the introduction to this section, we talked about a theory that a person under stress would be more likely to act aggressively if that person had often seen aggression as a solution. That hypothesis is difficult to test directly. But if the hypothesis is correct, there must be a correlation between preference for TV violence and later aggression. If that correlation were *not* present, the hypothesis of a causal relationship would be indefensible. The presence of the correlation is evidence for, but not "absolute proof" of, a causal relationship.

The investigators were interested in looking for a causal link, even though they were aware that their design did not control for other sources of influence on aggression. They performed a correlational analysis, called "path analysis," and concluded that their data *were* consistent with a causal interpretation. This analysis allowed the investigators to rule out as possible causes the other factors measured: IQ, parental personality, socioeconomic status, and others.

Let's return to the original question of this section. These investigators have provided information useful to any scientist interested in the possible role of thousands of hours of TV watching, especially of watching violence, in influencing aggressive behavior. If stress results in aggressive behavior in some children and adults, and not in others, these data point to one possible explanation of the question, Why.

WHAT DOES COMPLETE ISOLATION DO TO PERSONALITY?

The question of why personality changes under stress has been explored from several different vantage points. Now we would like to look at a definition of the term *stress* that is radically different from the preceding meanings. To do this, we will pose the question, What are the effects on personality of an environment that is so bare the person is left with essentially nothing to see, hear, feel, smell, or taste—and nothing to do? That is, What are the effects of *sensory deprivation*?

Perhaps you have never thought about it in these terms, but if a person is to function reasonably normally, it helps a great deal if the environment provides at least some stimulation. The expression, "it helps a great deal," may be an understatement. We shall see. You may have found yourself at one time or another in a situation that was so boring you noticed sharp differences in yourself. You may have been much more irritable than usual. You may have found yourself talking or singing to yourself, or looking for things to do that you would not even have considered under normal circumstances, such as watching a *terrible* TV program. There are instances of relatively complete and prolonged sensory deprivation. You may have read about the strange effects on people of the monotony encountered during exploration of the polar icecaps. Or you may have read about problems encountered on long, solitary sea voyages that some undertake voluntarily and that others are forced to undertake because of shipwreck. Another severe deprivation condition is solitary confinement in prison. While high levels of light energy or sound energy may be present in these situations, there is virtually no change in the input, no environmental variability, which is the essence of stimulation. The psychological effects of such prolonged social isolation and prolonged lack of environmental variation are extraordinary. Some people have come out of deprivation experiences with serious emotional disturbances. Almost all have reported experiencing serious disturbances of psychological functions while under such conditions. They have commonly reported hallucinations (seeing, hearing, or feeling "things" that are not there), delusions (false beliefs, such as the belief that one has just communicated with the dead or that one has just discovered the key to the great mysteries of the universe), inability to perform routine tasks, inability to concentrate, and so forth.

Perhaps you have also read about or seen movies about a phenomenon with the sinister name of *brainwashing*. Brainwashing may seem unrelated to the above, but the relationship will become clear. In fact, sensory deprivation may be an important ingredient of brainwashing.

Many people were surprised and disturbed at reports coming out of Russia in the 1950s concerning trials of some purged, political figures. The Russians were getting obviously false, even bizarre, confessions from these people and getting them in public trials. Perhaps most surprising was the behavior of the defendants. Formerly fiery party leaders were now docile, passive men. Bears had become lambs. What new, powerful means of producing personality changes did the Russians have? Also, reports of even more far-reaching programs of thought reform were coming out of Communist China, but these received relatively little publicity. The events that really upset the American public were the accounts after the Korean War of the seemingly absolute control that the Communist Chinese and North Koreans were able to achieve over American prisoners of war. At this time the word *brainwashing* became popular in the English language. The Red Chinese were effecting radical revisions in personality. *How* was not understood. Many soldiers were unprepared to cope with the methods, whatever they were.

And here begins the scientific tale. In the early 1950s, D. O. Hebb of McGill University initiated research into stimulus conditions associated with brainwashing and with losses of attention in situations calling for prolonged vigilance. Hebb theorized that the extraordinary alterations in behavior were perhaps the results of an extraordinarily monotonous environment. This seemed possible, considering that changes in the beliefs, perceptions, and feelings of many individiuals had been temporarily brought about by the natural deprivation conditions on solitary sea voyages, and other such situations. Hebb did not "just happen" to be the scientist who saw the relationship. He had just published a major theoretical book, *The Organization of Behavior* (1949), in which he had concluded that some minimal level of sensory input was necessary for the maintenance of normal thought, feeling, emotion, and so forth. Therefore, he argued, severe restriction of sensory input would have serious consequences for the person. Perhaps this was the key to the profound personality changes associated with brainwashing.

Hebb decided that a proper understanding of the relationship between sensory isolation and personality change could best be attained through experimentation. That is, he decided to manipulate the environment systematically in order to create deprivation. There are important reasons for studying the question experimentally. If you compare a naturally existing environment involving severe deprivation to a normally stimulating environment, the two differ in many ways. Unless the environment is brought under the control of the experimenter, it is impossible to tell which difference or combination of differences produces behavioral change.

In the naturally occurring deprivation situations, there is not only prolonged lack of environmental variability but also factors such as prolonged social isolation, frequently prolonged restriction of activity, and disruption of sleep cycles. Furthermore, all of these are complex in themselves. Hebb and his colleagues began the task of trying to specify just what it was in these situations that led to the changes in behavior. In other words, they set out to identify what aspects of these situations constituted *stress*.

The first experimental study of sensory deprivation was performed at

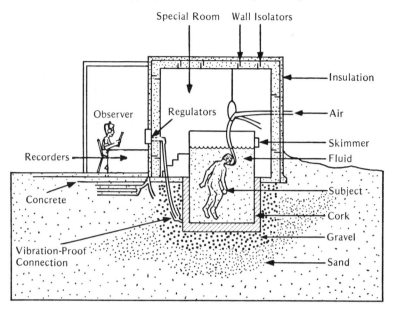

Figure 1. Schematic elevation of experimental sensory isolation laboratory.

McGill University by Hebb's colleagues. They paid male college students twenty dollars per day to do *nothing!* All they had to do was to lie on a bed all day and night, with their eyes and hands covered, and with all meaningful sounds masked by a loud electric air conditioner. They became upset. They hallucinated. They had delusions. Their performance on various tests suffered, and generally they could tolerate the situation for only a couple of days. This was the first experiment in the area, and it is extremely interesting research. We will, however, concentrate on a study that was performed after the McGill research, one that manipulated sensory deprivation in a far more complete fashion.

In 1960, Jay T. Shurley, a professor of psychiatry at the University of Oklahoma School of Medicine, published a report entitled, "Profound Experimental Sensory Isolation."

Shurley's definition of sensory isolation—that is, the experimental operation that he performed—reduced the level of stimulation to as nearly absolute deprivation as seems possible (see Figure 1).

He had a special room-within-a-room constructed. In the interior room there was a well, lined with a thick layer of cork. In that well was a tank, cut off from sources of mechanical or sound vibration in the outside world. The tank was filled with slowly flowing water maintained at a constant temperature of 93.5° Fahrenheit. The subject was suspended in the water, clad only in a mask that permitted effortless breathing of pure, odor-free, constant-temperature air and was instructed to restrict body movement as much as possible. Thus the subject was immersed in an environment that was as close as one can get to the total absence of stimulation. The subject experienced not only a uniform tactual field and unchanging temperature, but also had visual and auditory stimuli closed out by the tank and mask. The subject was given nothing to eat while in the tank, and the senses of taste, smell, touch, vision, and hearing were deprived of even remotely normal levels of stimulation. Furthermore, the mask was carefully weighted so that the subject's buoyancy was neutral, removing even the normal gravity cues. All of the stimulation you constantly get from the muscles and joints of your body when you are walking or when you are standing still maintaining an upright posture were gone. Thus Shurley created the situation that he used as the definition of sensory isolation, or in our terms *stress*.

What behaviors did he use to measure personality change? Up to now we have considered experiments in which the investigators utilized a precise, narrow specification of some behavior to define personality change. Shurley simply observed and recorded what the subjects said. Objectivity of observation was assured by the recordings of the subjects' verbalizations. The record of the behavior was kept so that it could be made available for "public" observation. Some subjects reported their experiences as they were undergoing them by talking into a microphone in the mask. Others gave reports from memory of what they had experienced in the tank. Full and open reporting was encouraged by guarantees of anonymity. And so the subjects talked! They talked about what they "saw," what they "heard," and what they "felt."

No subject stayed in the tank for more than six hours. Paradoxically, all were willing to undergo the profound isolation again, despite the fact that their normal perceptual and intellectual functions had been completely distorted. What Shurley called "mental imagery," including dreams and hallucinations, occurred in the visual, auditory, kinesthetic (which means pertaining to stimulation from the muscles and tendons), and olfactory senses. The best way to communicate in any real way how the subjects changed in the isolation condition is to do what Shurley did—to present a verbatim transcript of part of a subject's report. The following is from a twenty-nine-year-old man, a journalist:

In the second hour his comments concerned his self-thwarted, increasing urgency for "exercise" and physical activity; amazement at his lack of appetite for a cigarette; his state of utter loneliness and solitude, save for "my very real companions, my thoughts and memories"; compassion for the little space-monkey, Sam, who received only half an apple and a glass of water for his dinner after his historic trip 55 miles into space; thoughts of food and sudden, intense hunger pangs.

He whistled, and then sang the refrain from a popular tune which went, "I'll never get rid of that ------, -------, --------!" Apparently he dropped off into a short (less than two minutes) nap; he woke with a start and the eerie feeling he had just been "out of this world," and with a very vivid, "long" dream, which he struggled to recall. He succeeded in recalling only a part—"a sawdust cream cone."

In the third hour he questioned and then asserted he heard the very faint sound of water trickling (the tape records the sound); asserted he heard dogs barking (not present on the tape); and commented on a "crackling sound" (unable to verify from the tape). At intervals he sang, increasingly louder, the refrain from a slightly obscene ditty which began, "Roll me over . . . "

Increasingly strong impulses to action came: "I had an urge to make like a porpoise, but those darned hoses (air supply) won't let me!" Briefly, he seemed to be in quite an ebullient, elated mood. Suddenly, he plunged into grief and tears with the expressed thought, "How many people really think about what it's all about? How many people ever, ever think—just once—about love?"

Within seconds, the depressed mood vanished and he was again joking, whistling, and laughing. A make-believe dialogue ensued, as he asked, anxiously, "Joe, what do you do when your engine quits at 200 feet?" and replied, in a peal of laughter, "You land the sonofabitch!"

Immediately following, his tone shifted and he uttered an angry command: "You voice! Keep quiet up there! Quiet!" He, himself, obeyed, and was silent, but only briefly. He hummed. He sang. He sighed deeply. He yawned. He seemed unutterably bored.

His thoughts turned to his plan to compose his report and his budget, and the belated recognition he had not even begun to accomplish this. In a half-hearted explanation to himself, he said, "I just allowed my thoughts to drift." Futility and resignation hung from his tone of voice. He then remarked briskly, "I seem kind of wide awake. I ought to get out!" For a period following this, there was more singing, more humming. Then "I don't know, but it seems like I heard voices. Somewhere. Male voices. Men's voices. Too bad! (laughter) It should have been a bunch of dollies!" He laughed again. More singing came.

In a tone of extreme annoyance, he blurted out, "I might just as well be Sam, for all I can be or do or think or hear or be or smell or taste!"

Over the next 10 minutes he argued himself into the position that he was "just wasting time. After all, I feel fine." "This is ridiculous" (here he referred to his being a grown man bobbing around in the dark in a tank of water in a hole under the hospital). "Besides," he added, "this run isn't producing any data for the doctor, anyway!"

Again, he commented and questioned whether he really was hearing "some noises." Abruptly, he pulled off the mask and left the tank (Shurley, 1960, pp. 541–542).

One woman reported "seeing" several marvelous hallucinations, including a full-color, three-dimensional view of a "field of golden toadstools standing in bright sunlight." She also "saw" herself as an iced-tea spoon, slowly stirring a glass of iced tea. She woke up to find her left leg moving in a circular stirring motion! (Shurley, 1962). Other subjects reported seeing the experimenter through the walls of the tank, seeing patterns of brilliant lights, smelling garlic, smelling hot tar. One "heard" his name called by his father's voice. Other subjects reported unusual attentional effects. A physician reported hearing not only his heartbeat but also the snapping shut of his aortic valve. Another physician reported "in awe" that he could hear the gliding sounds of his own skeletal joints as he moved. When the experimenter had to leave one subject for a few minutes, interrupting the postexperimental interview, he returned only to find the subject carrying on a rather animated interview with himself, both asking and answering questions.

There was, in short, a wide range of alterations in the behavior of the sensorially isolated and deprived subjects.

Shurley set out with a question about "the nature and range of psychophysiological phenomena evoked in intact humans experimentally exposed in solitude to an environment which profoundly diminishes absolute amounts of sensory inputs . . . " (1960, p. 539). He created such an environment and recorded what happened.

Shurley's study reflects a research strategy that involves asking a question almost at the level of the operations. It is a "what would happen if we did this" type of question, and very little reduction was involved in going from the original question to the research study itself. This is in sharp contrast to research like Hunt's, which began with a theoretical question about the effects of frustration in infancy and wound up studying the hoarding behavior of rats.

While Shurley's question was at the level of operations and involved relatively little reduction, it was asked in the context of a much broader question. How does brainwashing work? The research of Hebb, Shurley, and others, and the reports of former prisoners point to one important factor. That factor is sensory isolation. Whether sensory isolation per se is a form of stress is an interesting question, left open by the Shurley research. Earlier researchers had interpreted the effects as indicating stress. We will return to this question in Part III.

CAN CONFLICT CAUSE NEUROSIS?

ou are all to some extent familiar with the term *neurosis*. Generally, this term refers to problems in personality adjustment that are not serious enough to require hospitalization but which cause a good deal of discomfort. In many textbooks neurosis or neurotic behavior is viewed as a reaction to stress. That is, in oversimplified terms, the person experiences some form of stress, and this stress affects personality by leading to maladaptive behavior patterns that are termed neurotic.

"Neurotic" behavior has many different definitions. However, most psychologists would agree on some general forms of behavior that characterize neurosis. Behaviors that are not appropriate to the situation, are very difficult to change, and persist even in the face of punishment are usually labeled neurotic. For example, a person may develop a paralysis without any physiological basis and never walk again, even though such behavior may cost him or her a job and all opportunities for normal social interaction. Or a person may fear the opposite sex so much that he or she forms no heterosexual relationships, at the cost of being lonely and unhappy.

Psychiatrists and psychologists have long observed these kinds of behaviors. There are many theories as to why neurotic people behave as they do. But these theories are largely untested in the scientific sense. Our understanding of neuroses is far from complete, primarily because this aspect of human behavior is extremely difficult to study. Clearly we cannot perform on people experimental manipulations that might lead to persistent, maladaptive behavior. Furthermore, an extremely wide variety of behaviors define neurosis. Multitudes of factors would have to be controlled if we were to approach the question experimentally. Think for a moment about all of the things that might influence the development of neurotic behavior, such as child-rearing practices, socioeconomic status, geographic area, genetic endowment, family size, and constitutional factors like body build. Primarily because of these reasons, the animal laboratory has supplied much of the experimentally derived data aimed at clarifying the conditions under which neurosis develops. Of course, the experimenters have had to direct their research toward limited aspects of the problem. They have had to reduce this complex issue to the point of asking very narrow questions. Thus the answers are also very limited, especially in view of the magnitude of the "real-life" problem. The research to be discussed in the present section is an excellent example of this reduction.

Experimenters have long observed that under certain stress situations, animals manifest behavior that bears resemblances to human neurotic behavior. In fact, as long ago as the 1920s, Pavlov termed such behavior "experimental neurosis." Researchers saw in these behaviors the opportunity to examine the development of neurosis ethically and under well-controlled conditions. For the past forty years, there have been numerous efforts to study experimental neurosis, using a variety of animals as subjects.

As we have seen in the section discussing Hunt's research, Freud and his followers developed a theory of behavior that proposed that neurosis develops, at least in part, out of the traumatic experiences of childhood. Freud's theory is elaborate and difficult to test experimentally. Nevertheless, some basic principles deriving from psychoanalytic thought have become extremely important in the experimental investigation of behavior. In 1943, a psychiatrist by the name of Jules H. Masserman published a book entitled *Behavior and Neurosis*. In this book he outlined some of these basic Freudian principles that guided his own study of experimental neurosis. The four basic principles, paraphrasing Masserman (pp. 7–8), follow.

1. *Behavior is fundamentally motivated by the needs of the organism.* These needs may be termed "instincts" as in Freud's works, or "goal-directed striving," or whatever; the principle still holds.

2. *Behavior is contingent upon the demands of the environment and represents an adaptation between the individual and his or her changing surroundings.* This means that behavior is dependent upon people's interests, needs, and potentials, and how these interact with the environment. Also implicit in this principle is the idea that between these two broad classes of determinants (the person and his or her environment), people in some way manage to form adaptive relationships with the world.

3. *Behavior is not always a simple and direct satisfying of elementary needs.* Behavior includes thoughts, gestures, and words.

4. *The motivations of behavior may become conflicted when two or more needs are aroused at the same time and when the satisfaction of one of these needs necessarily prevents satisfaction of the others.* We have all experienced this state of affairs at least in relatively mild forms. For example, you want to have a rich dessert but you are already overweight. This last principle is the most important one for present purposes. Masserman argued that neurotic behavior results from being in a situation that produces conflicts between drives or needs. He devoted a large portion of his book to experiments in which animals are subjected to different forms of conflict, and he described the resultant changes in behavior.

Masserman proposed that the principles summarized above lead to the following manipulations necessary for laboratory investigations of experimental neurosis:

1. *Producing or activating a strong biological drive.* For example, depriving an animal of food.

2. *Associating some stimulus with the conditions surrounding the satisfaction of that drive.* That is, presenting a tone to the animal just prior to feeding It.

3. *Arranging the situation so that the animal is in conflict regarding the satisfaction of the drive.* At the time of reinforcement (food delivery), shocking the animal. The animal can eat, but is shocked if it does.

4. *Observing the effects of this conflict.* Examining the animal's behavior at the time of conflict and observing responses to the signal that has been associated with the conflict situation.

Let us now look at his actual research.

Masserman used cats as subjects. He manipulated hunger drive by depriving the cats of food, thus accomplishing the first of the steps just outlined. He then associated a stimulus with the eating response. To do this, it was first necessary to train the cats to make a specific response with which the stimulus could be associated. This was done by putting the hungry cat in a test cage containing a food box but no food. Food was then placed in the box and the animal was allowed to eat. A signal (a light plus a bell) was presented when the food was placed in the box. After a series of such trials, animals quickly came to the food box and ate when the signal was presented. Food was delivered *only* after the signal.

The next step in the training of a specific response was to teach the animals to lift a lid on the food box to obtain food each time the signal occurred. This was accomplished by lowering the lid on the box more and more as trials progressed. That is, each time the signal was presented, the cats were required to increase their head contact with the box lid. Eventually the lid was completely closed and the cats had learned to lift the lid with their heads to get food in response to the signals. The second major step had been accomplished; animals were associating eating with an external stimulus.

Then it was necessary to produce the conflict situation. After animals were trained to lift the food box lid and eat *in response to the light-bell signal*, some received an aversive air-blast just at the moment of feeding. Others received shock through the floor of the cage just as they began to eat. Still others received a combination of air and shock right at this crucial time. Thus two needs were pitted against one another, the drive to eat and the need to avoid or escape the undesirable stimulation.

It would be useful to recall at this point the discussion of constructs in Part I. Masserman conceptualized this experiment in terms of internal states of the organism. He was concerned with *internal* conflict, *internal* stress. But this experiment illustrates clearly that it is not *necessary* to do so and may be conceptually simpler *not* to do so. The conflict situation, which is the form of stress under consideration, can be objectively defined by the external conditions in which the cats were placed. That is, we can talk about the antecedents of the cats' neurotic behavior in terms of the deprivation of food and the air blast. The data can be used, as Masserman used them, to theorize about the role of inferred internal states, or we can "stay outside the cat," as we have chosen to do. Similarly, the term *neurosis* might call up in your thinking something like an "internal disease." It need not. Again, we can elect to stay at the level of whatever maladaptive behavior the cat exhibits. Labeling the behavior "experimental neurosis" may be convenient, but it may also lead us astray in thinking about that behavior. You should note that we will stay at the level of objectively describable manipulations and objectively observable behavior, in the analysis of this research itself. If it is correct that this type of stress produces the experimental neurosis, then these cats should show marked behavior changes that are persistent and maladaptive.

Masserman reports that there were great individual differences in the way his cats reacted. He was able to categorize the behavior changes into four types of reactions: (1) changes in spontaneous activity, (2) "phobic" responses to feeding signals, (3) "counterphobic" behavior patterns, and (4) "regressive" behavior. Let us examine two of these categories of neurotic behavior more closely.

As for changes in spontaneous activity, Masserman noted that animals which had been generally quiet and not very active in the feeding situation became "restless or agitated" after experiencing the conflict. For example, "cat 53 was a normally quiet animal in which two blasts of air abolished further feeding responses but produced a fidgety, incessant pacing and shifting from side to side . . . and characteristic postures and acting . . . (which mimicked) anxiety" (p. 67). On the other hand, animals that were generally active during the feeding situation became remarkably quiet and passive. "Cats 14 and 52 were highly excitable and easily distractible animals, which reacted with frenzied leaping at the air-blasts but which thereafter refused to feed with food easily available and lay passive and immobile between feeding signals in any portion of the cage in which they were placed" (p. 67).

You have probably heard of *phobias*. A phobia is a neurotic reaction that is fairly common and refers to extreme fear associated with objects or situations such as fear of heights and closed places. Some of Masserman's cats developed responses to the feeding signals that seemed to be like phobic behavior in humans. Animals that normally rushed to the food box following the feeding signal now responded by crouching, hiding, attempting to escape the cage, and showing signs of extreme fear. They trembled and appeared to panic. In some cases these responses lasted for months even in the absence of air-blasts or shocks.

Thus the cats did develop persistent and maladaptive responses that could be termed neurotic. Masserman raised the question of whether these responses were due to the conflict, or to the other operations involved in the experiment. That is, could the presentation of the light-bell stimulus itself produce the changes? Could a simple pairing of these stimuli with air blasts "cause" a neurosis? These and other questions had to be answered before the results could be interpreted unambiguously. Therefore, Masserman carried out a series of control experiments. None of them produced the neurotic behaviors that he had observed in the experiment involving conflict. The data from the control experiments strongly support Masserman's argument that it was the conflict in the situation that produced the experimental neurosis. However, this is only part of the story. Masserman also asked the question, Is it possible to give these cats "psychotherapy" and eliminate the experimentally induced neurosis? He conducted six experiments to examine the conditions under which the persistent, maladaptive behavior patterns may be eliminated or reduced. Let us examine three of these.

First, thirty-seven neurotic cats were returned to the experimental situation after *rest periods* varying from two weeks to five months after the development of the neurosis. Thirty of these animals demonstrated neurotic behavior that was just as severe as it was on the last day of the experimental procedure that constituted stress. Rest alone was not effective.

Next, Masserman tried what he called "reduction of one of the conflictual drives." Neurotic cats that were force-fed just before being returned to the experimental cage usually showed significant reductions in neurotic behavior when the feeding signal was presented. It is important to note, however, that it was not possible to reinstate the normal feeding response to the light-bell signal when animals were placed in the test cage while hungry. In fact, as soon as the hunger was reestablished by depriving the cats of food, the cats again displayed neurotic behavior in response to the feeding signal.

Another attempt to provide psychotherapy for the animals was to *place a normal cat*, that is, one that had not been subjected to the experimental procedure and had exhibited no unusual behaviors, *in the experimental situation with a neurotic one*. Each neurotic cat was put into the test cage with a cat trained to eat to the feeding signal. This was partially successful. In some cases the behavior of the nonneurotic animals eventually led the neurotic subjects to eat in response to the signal. In some cases normal behavior was reinstated. In other cases, the neurotic cat ate in response to the signal only hesitantly and irregularly, while still other neurotic animals failed to reestablish the normal eating response even after numerous trials over a two-week period.

While it is apparent that Masserman was able to effect some "cures" by instituting procedures aimed at reducing the basic conflict involved, in no case was treatment 100 percent effective. The therapeutic procedures were more effective than the rest-period operation, that is, more effective than no therapy at all. Those treatments that were aimed at reducing or abolishing conflict were the most successful.

Masserman presents data that indicate that the best therapy may be starving the animal and placing the cat within sight and smell of the food. This has the effect of reducing the conflict because the hunger drive becomes so much stronger than the tendency to avoid the food box. He also points out that a combination of therapies would probably be best for any one neurotic cat.

What does this research have to say about our original question, Why does a person's personality change under stress? Masserman has demonstrated that certain behavioral changes in cats, which he calls "neurotic," resulted from a stress situation that produced conflict between motives. It has been pointed out several times already, that such a demonstration allows us to look for similar relationships in situations where experimental manipulations are impossible. It should also be pointed out, however, that these experiments have *not* demonstrated that the changes recorded are the *only* ones. They are the ones that the investigator focused upon. Nor has it been demonstrated that *only* stress situations producing conflict will lead to the changes noted. The investigator has ruled out other aspects of his experiment that might have led to the experimental neurosis. There may be a wide variety of other sources of experimental neurosis not addressed in Masserman's study.

IS THERE A PSYCHOPHYSIOLOGICAL REASON FOR EXPERIMENTAL NEUROSIS?

e have seen that stresses of different kinds lead to a variety of observable changes in the behavior of people and animals. Sometimes the changes produced in laboratories are maladaptive, manifest themselves outside of the actual experimental situation, and persist after the stress is gone. These, as we have seen, are *experimental neuroses.* Masserman's research provides one example, but there are many others. Sheep, dogs, goats, rats, pigs, and primates, as well as cats, have been subjects in similar experiments. Behavioral changes have ranged from minor responses such as facial twitches (or tics) to wholesale personality changes in the animals.

Thus the experimental neurosis research deals with a question of potentially great significance, What are the essential conditions leading to the lasting disturbances in behavior we call "experimental neurosis"? If we can specify them in the laboratory, perhaps we'll know where to look in the natural environment for the conditions giving rise to human neurosis. This is the hope so often expressed by the laboratory investigator.

Before beginning his own research, Masserman searched through the published reports of other experimenters' work and concluded that the crucial element leading to experimental neurosis was some manipulation producing *conflict.* He arrived at this hypothesis by examining the manipulations that had been used by other investigators, but he had a particular theoretical orientation guiding his reading. In the study we shall describe in this section, Johnson (1963) also arrived at his hypothesis by examining the literature on experimental neurosis. Instead of trying to abstract the common thread from the manipulations, Johnson tried to determine what was common to the various theoretical constructs that had been used to explain the behavior change. He was impressed with the fact that while many of the researchers employed procedures (such as shock) from which fear or anxiety would normally be inferred, many other researchers did not use such procedures.

Johnson hypothesized that experimental neurosis might be explained by a construct that had found wide usage in the study of motivation—*arousal*. In his words, "It is suggested here that the use of such terms as *fear* and *anxiety* do not adequately describe the phenomenon (of experimental neurosis) and that the evidence is more clearly understood if one thinks in terms of physiological arousal rather than in terms of anxiety or fear which imply some real or perceived threat to the organism" (p. 116). In Part I we noted that we would use the term *construct* to refer to a set of related observable behaviors, or related manipulations. This is an exception. "Arousal" as defined above, and as used in the literature, is truly a physiological state, measurable by physiological means.

Johnson contended that all of the experimental manipulations used in experimental neurosis research cause high levels of physiological arousal, which "eventually result in the breakdown of the animal" (p. 115). Arousal refers to a construct having a variety of behavioral referents. For example, the individual who is highly aroused may be extremely alert. If too highly aroused, the individual may be tense and overresponsive and may behave inappropriately. Highly aroused persons may appear to be very anxious or disorganized. Arousal is measured by heart rate, brain waves, respiration rate, skin conductance, and so forth. These measures of physiological functioning—which can be taken from *outside* the organism and which the investigator is attempting to relate to such behaviors as tenseness, disorganization, and others—are called *psychophysiological measures*. If Masserman's goal was to relate experimental neurosis to the construct of conflict, Johnson's goal can be seen as an attempt to relate experimental neurosis to the construct of arousal.

The specific goal of this particular study is narrower than that of Masserman's. Johnson wanted to show that a typical experimental neurosis manipulation (a difficult discrimination task) would produce a change in certain measures of physiological arousal. His intent was to "demonstrate the existence of high levels of arousal brought about by difficult discrimination tasks" (p. 116). As you look closely at his experiment, keep in mind that he was looking for evidence that arousal was the key factor in the development of experimental neurosis.

The subjects were sixty female students in an introductory psychology course. While they were required to participate in a number of experiments as a part of the course, the only students who served in this experiment were those who agreed to do so after a one-second test shock, which was of the same strength and duration as that used throughout the experiment. The subjects were divided into four groups, two "experimental" and two "control." All of the subjects participated for three 50-minute sessions, during which continuous recordings were made of their heart rates, skin conductances, and palmar sweat (the latter two being measures of perspiration). The experimental operations (procedures) defining the four groups were as follows.

Difficult discrimination group. Each of the fifteen subjects in this experimental group was seated in a comfortable chair and hooked up to the recording apparatus by recording electrodes. The subject rested an index finger on a lever and had a shock electrode taped to that finger. Her task in the first of the three sessions was to respond to a signal, a 2-second presentation of a metronome beating at 144 beats per minute, by lifting her finger off the switch. If she failed to respond, she got a mild shock. If, however, the 2-second metronome signal was at a frequency of 60 beats per minute, she would get shocked if she *lifted* her finger but would avoid shock by keeping her finger where it was. This procedure is diagrammed below.

FAST BEAT	LIFT	NO SHOCK
FAST BEAT	NO LIFT	SHOCK
SLOW BEAT	LIFT	SHOCK
SLOW BEAT	NO LIFT	NO SHOCK

In the second session the same procedure was used, except that during the session the slow beat was made faster and faster until it became so similar to the fast beat that the subjects began making errors. In other words, they had difficulty discriminating between the two beats. In the third session, the discrimination problem remained very difficult for the subjects, except for the last five trials, which were made easy so that subjects would not leave the experiment feeling agitated.

Impossible discrimination group. This group was treated in the same way as the difficult discrimination group for the first two sessions. In the third session, however, the discrimination was made impossible by increasing the slow beat to 144 beats per minute! On some of the trials, the experimenter considered the 144-beat stimulus to be the fast one and punished the failure to respond. On the other trials, he considered the 144-beat stimulus to be the slow beat and punished the responses.

Control groups. To rule out the possibility that changes in arousal occurring over the course of the experiment may have been due to the shock itself, a control group was yoked to the difficult discrimination group. Each subject in this control group was paired with a subject in the difficult discrimination group and heard a 144-beat tone as often as her counterpart in the experimental group, but she never heard the other tone. She also got a shock every time her counterpart got one.

The subjects in this control group were therefore unable to discriminate between shock and nonshock trials.

In order to eliminate any possibility that changes in arousal might be due simply to the effects of unpredictability of shock, another control group was employed. Subjects in the other groups were unable to predict without error when they would get shocked. To rule this out as an explanation, each subject in this second control group was yoked to a subject in the impossible discrimination group and got shocked as often as did her experimental counterpart. This control group, however, heard the 144-beat signal *only* on those occasions prior to receiving shock. Thus, there was no uncertainty aroused by the signal; when they heard it, they knew that they were about to get shocked. And they never got shocked without a signal.

The control groups, then, were treated identically with the experimental groups except that neither of the control groups could avoid shock by discriminating appropriately between signals. Their responses could not prevent shock. The second control group had no uncertainty about when shock would occur. You will notice that there has been a great emphasis placed upon controlling for the effects of shock. There is a very important reason for this. Since Johnson was interested in studying arousal as a function of difficult discrimination, he had to pay particular attention to other factors that might produce arousal. Shock is a potent source of arousal.

As you will see, another way to think about the function of the control subjects in this experiment is as a baseline group with which to compare whatever changes may occur in the experimental subjects.

It is well known among investigators who use these psychophysiological measures that subjects get used to the experiment and to whatever stimulation they are receiving. The psychophysiological measures gradually habituate; that is, they return slowly to a point close to their "normal" level. Since the effects of habituation are in the opposite direction of the expected effects of the experimenter's manipulation, the crucial evaluation of the data is a test of whether or not the groups *change differently* over the course of the experiment. In fact, the groups did change differently. For the experimental groups, the heart rate scores increased slightly overall but increased fairly sharply from session two to session three. Conversely, the heart rates of the control groups decreased over the course of the experiment. Therefore, the requirement that the subjects make difficult or impossible discriminations to avoid shock had a greater effect on the heart rate than did an equivalent amount of shock alone. Similar results were found with the skin conductance and the palmar sweat measures. The statistical analyses of the data showed that the groups changed differently over time. A study of the graphs presented by Johnson reveals that the experimental subjects responded differently from the controls, and the major difference occurred between the second and third sessions. The control groups continued to display a decrease in arousal. The experimental subjects, especially the impossible discrimination group, increased most at that point.

Johnson sums up his interpretation of his results as follows: "All of the results of this study seem to indicate that the effects of experimental neurosis paradigms might best be phrased in terms of increases in physiological arousal rather than in terms of fear of anxiety responses" (p. 123).

Look back at the operations used in the third session for the impossible discrimination group. Compare them with the first control group discussed. They are identical. Both groups heard only the 144-beat tone; both were able to move their finger off the key; but both were, in fact, helpless to avoid shock. Yet, their behavior was radically different, as measured psychophysiologically. An observer trying to make sense out of the experimental operations with only the third session to examine would be bewildered. What was different about these two groups in the third session? The subjects in the impossible discrimination group brought to session three a two-session history of success in avoiding shock. They had learned that they could control what was going to happen by making the appropriate responses to the noticeably different stimuli. However, the control subjects had, from the outset of the experiment, been completely unable to exert any control over whether they would get shocked or not. In essence, they were not trying. Any interpretation of experimental results must always take into account what the *subject* is trying to do in the experimental situation. A moment's reflection on the research performed by Miller on the acquisition, or learning, of fear will suffice to reinforce this point. Whether or not a situation is stressful for a given organism will very likely depend upon the history of that organism.

Now let's place the study back into the context of Johnson's larger question. While Johnson's broad purpose was to isolate a crucial factor underlying the development of experimental neurosis, if we stick to the level of the data, he demonstrated that forcing a human female subject to make difficult discriminations to avoid shock had a rather great influence on several measures of arousal. This study is a made-to-order example of what was said earlier about taking a question and breaking it down into answerable pieces. It is but one small step in the direction of establishing that arousal is central to the development of experimental neurosis. What would have to be done further to establish that contention? First, all of the experimental operations that lead to experimental neurosis would have to be investigated in a similar manner. It would have to be demonstrated that all of them do in fact result in high levels of physiological arousal. It would then have to be demonstrated that, under some conditions, high levels of physiological arousal will ultimately lead to the kinds of sustained behavioral alterations that define experimental neurosis. You should keep in mind that this was *not* demonstrated in the study just reported. Also remember the implication that arousal need not lead to experimental neurosis under all conditions. Other conditions may channel the effects of arousal toward some other form of behavioral change. In sum, in order to firmly establish the relationship between arousal and experimental neurosis, the conditions under which arousal does and does not lead to experimental neurosis would have to be carefully and completely delineated.

CAN FEAR KILL?

p to now we have focused primarily upon laboratory experimentation as the way in which researchers have tried to answer questions about the relationships between stress and personality. These investigators have attempted to manipulate conditions, to objectify observations, and to quantify their results as much as possible. We have seen how elaborate control operations have been used and how experimenters have attempted to rule out alternative explanations of their findings.

We are now going to examine a bit of research which, in the formal experimental sense, does none of these things and yet in one way or another does many of them. We are going to see how W. B. Cannon (1942) attempted to use reports from observers of numerous cultures plus data from the laboratory to interpret a fascinating phenomenon, "voodoo" death.

For centuries, students of so-called primitive cultures have observed deaths that on the surface appear to be caused by black magic. These voodoo deaths have occurred in various parts of the world: South America, South Africa, Australia, New Zealand, Haiti, and the Pacific Islands. The magical means by which they are supposedly accomplished take various forms. In some areas if the victims discover they have eaten a taboo, but not poisonous, food, they may die soon afterward. In other areas if the victims hear that a death curse has been placed upon them by a witch or shaman, the voodoo deaths occur. In other cases if a magician points a certain kind of bone at the victim, the victim literally wastes away and dies within a matter of days.

These are recorded "facts." A good description of such events is given by Cannon, who quoted an on-the-spot observer of this phenomenon, Dr. Herbert Basedow, a student of primitive Australian cultures. Dr. Basedow stated:

The man who discovers that he is being boned by any enemy is, indeed, a pitiable sight. He stands aghast, with his eyes staring at the treacherous pointer, and with his hands lifted as though to ward off the lethal medium, which he imagines is pouring into his body. His cheeks blanch and his eyes become glassy and the expression of his face becomes horribly distorted . . . he attempts to shriek but usually the sound chokes in his throat, and all that one might see is froth at his mouth. His body begins to tremble and the muscles twist involuntarily. He sways backwards and falls to the ground, and after a short time appears to be in a swoon but soon after he writhes as if in mortal agony, and, covering his face with his hands begins to moan. After a while he becomes very composed and crawls to his wurley. From this time onwards he sickens and frets, refusing to eat and keeping aloof from the daily affairs of the tribe. Unless help is forthcoming in the shape of a countercharm administered by the hands of the Nangarri, or medicine-man, his death is only a matter of a comparatively short time. If the coming of the medicine-man is opportune he might be saved. (Cannon, p. 172)

The course of events is similar from place to place. Individuals who have been cursed are convinced they will die. Enemies, friends, and relatives, too, believe death is at hand. They isolate themselves from their social environment, and others in their environment isolate them. They stop eating and drinking, and in a matter of days they die.

This may seem impossible. Since childhood most of us are told that witches do not exist and that magic is only make-believe. Everyone knows that magicians in our culture are really tricksters. But if this is true, how can we explain or understand voodoo death? One other question comes to mind: Are voodoo deaths due to natural causes? We know from the anthropological literature that primitive cultures try to make their world safer and more understandable by creating what seems to us to be strange explanations of natural phenomena. Perhaps disease, old age, or willful starvation may explain these mysterious deaths. Perhaps they are due to poison. If Cannon had been constructing a traditional experiment, he would have responded to these general questions by using controls. This was not possible. But he tried to achieve the functions of control—that is, he tried to rule out the above-stated, obvious, possible explanations of such events. How did he accomplish this? First of all, the possibility that old age is the most important determinant is ruled out by the fact that many victims were described as "young," "robust," and "strong." Starvation is ruled out by the rapidity with which death occurs. But how about disease as a major contributing factor? Here the evidence is quite certain. Medical examinations of dying victims (when available) revealed no physical illness. Likewise, available postmortem examinations revealed no physical cause of death. These findings are also relevant to the question about death by poisoning. That possibility was further ruled out since many of the cultures in which the voodoo deaths occurred were ignorant of the use of poison. In other cases, very few poisons were available. With these obvious explanations ruled out, then, the question is, can we find some scientifically acceptable reason for these events? Magic is not an acceptable explanation. Most scientists believe that explanations based on magic are really just ways of saying that we don't understand. It seems clear that something psychological is going on. In one recorded case, the witch had been forced to tell the victim that it was all a mistake, and the person suddenly got well.

How did Cannon go about determining just what psychological processes were operating? His first step was to try to discover under what common conditions the voodoo deaths occurred. Voodoo deaths are reported in superstitious, fear-ridden cultures. These are cultures in which the levels of education and technology are so primitive that it is quite possible for the people to believe unquestioningly that someone could actually kill by pointing a bone. Thus not only does the victim believe absolutely that bone pointing or other magic can kill, but everyone around believes the same. The victim acts and is treated by everyone as a dead person.

These conditions must be an extreme form of stress. This should be apparent if you think for a minute about how drastically your beliefs and the opinions of others can affect *your* emotional state. It seems reasonable to assume that social conditions are such that intense fear plays a major role in voodoo deaths. We might view the sequence in the following simplified manner: (1) The profound belief in death by magic, which is reinforced by the victim's environment, leads to (2) an intense fear that produces (3) profound physiological changes leading to severe physiological shock, (4) severe drops in blood pressure, and finally (5) death.

It appears to be common that once individuals have been doomed the people around them go through a two-stage social process. First, they withdraw *all* social support. They change all their attitudes toward them. The victims are now considered taboo. They are in a totally new and threatening situation. They are isolated. They are *alone*. This, in and of itself, is an extremely stressful situation, particularly in cultures where life itself is often dependent upon relationships with kin and tribal members.

In the second stage of this social process, the people around the victims begin to treat them as if they were already dead. They are mourned, and they mourn themselves. Thus the victims are in a social situation where deaths due to magic are as believable to them as deaths due to automobile accidents are to you. But is the *belief* that an event can kill really enough to *kill?* What physical steps actually cause death?

Cannon has been an important figure in physiology and particularly in the physiology of emotional behavior. It was thus normal that he should look to this level of investigation for an answer. He asked the question, Is it possible for intense fear to kill?

Here Cannon leaned heavily upon *previous* laboratory research to help him answer the question. He said that we know from past research that emotional arousal has profound effects upon physiological activity. The so-called sympathetic nervous system is highly involved in bodily functioning and affects the operation of the respiratory system, blood vessels, and major internal organs such as the heart.

Relatively long-term, intense, sympathetic functioning can clearly have "dire results," as Cannon put it.

In addition to this general knowledge from the results of animal research, Cannon knew that it might be possible for death to occur in a matter of hours under conditions of intense emotional stress. Researchers suggest that the extreme bodily responses observed in these kinds of deaths are much like those observed in the state of physiological shock attending physical injury. One major aspect of this type of shock is a drastic drop in blood pressure that is often fatal.

Thus, Cannon concluded, it is quite possible for intense fear to produce death. Now, how did this help Cannon arrive at a meaningful and scientifically acceptable answer to voodoo death? If fear can lead to death, then it is at least possible that the voodoo victim literally dies of fright.

Cannon studied this phenomenon outside of the laboratory, but his study is by no means just speculation. Cannon gathered his data thoroughly; he evaluated alternative explanations; he utilized sound research findings and from these "operations" deduced a scientifically meaningful explanation. But Cannon was not so naive as to believe that he had proven his contention. In fact, he pointed out that his conclusions were really nothing more than logically derived hypotheses and that other procedures could be used to test them. Researchers should attempt to obtain definitive physiological measures from voodoo victims, measures that would provide direct evidence of the presence or absence of physiological shock.

Beyond providing us with a hypothesis and a method for testing it, what else did Cannon do? He attempted to make scientific sense out of a phenomenon that is difficult to comprehend. To some extent, he demonstrated the tremendous potency of belief systems and how they may affect behavior. In this sense he said something we already know, but he said it in a very powerful manner. It's not just the particular external event that is stressful, but it is the event plus whatever meaning the event has for the individual. If an acquaintance pointed a bone at you and said you would die, you wouldn't drop dead; you would probably laugh. The difference between yourself and a person who would die of fright must be understood at two levels, the social and the biological.

Other investigators have taken generally large questions and have reduced them to the level of laboratory operations in attempts to provide a partial answer. Cannon also took on a large question. He did not reduce it by developing his own operations in an effort to provide the answer. He did, however, go through this reductionistic process. Part of his analysis was at the level of blood pressure drops in animals. He selected evidence that others had already provided through operations in the laboratory. In this way the process of reduction was carried out in spite of the fact that Cannon did not do an experiment.

Up to now we have been focusing on the first part of our grand question; that is, Why does one's personality change under stress? We are now going to address the second part of the question, How can psychologists help?

CAN PSYCHOLOGISTS HELP REDUCE CONFLICT BETWEEN PEOPLE?

onflict! That's a powerful word, calling up many images. Conflict is a major stress in any society. How can it be reduced? That is certainly part of the question, How can psychologists help?

The word *conflict* has many different meanings, but we are interested in discussing *interpersonal* conflict, conflict *between people*. Interpersonal conflict is often presented in the media as a life-and-death struggle. Who stays in the lifeboat? Who gets the remaining food? In our day-to-day lives, conflict is much more likely to be over less dramatic issues, such as a husband and wife arguing about how to spend the available money. Situations in which people agree on a goal but disagree on the means to achieve it are also common. Both parents may want their children to be independent but may disagree over how to encourage them to behave that way. We shall deal in this section with the question, How can we reduce interpersonal conflict?

There are limitations on our ability to think and communicate our thoughts to others. These include limitations on our ability to (a) know our own minds with respect to why we do what we do, (b) communicate what we think is important, (c) have our words agree with our actions, and (d) be consistent in our behavior from one time to another. If people really are deficient with respect to these abilities, just imagine the effects on conflict! These deficiencies must make existing conflict worse, creating doubts about each other's motives, and distrust in each other's words and deeds. If psychology can provide techniques to help overcome these limitations, then perhaps it can help people reach agreement with less conflict and stress. To provide part of an answer to the question, How can psychology help? let's consider a study by Balke, Hammond, and Meyer (1973).

The situation.　In 1970 a large chemical corporation underwent a long and bitter strike. The strike lasted over two months, imposing considerable financial hardship on both the company and the employees. Shortly after it was settled, the investigators were able to get three union negotiators and three management negotiators to serve in a research project. These six men were asked to reenact the negotiations that had finally led to the settlement of the strike. The researchers wanted to see if a *conflict reduction technique* that had been successfully used in the laboratory might help in the resolution of conflict in the real world.

An overview of the conflict reduction technique.   First, the underlying issues of conflict are identified by having the people involved list the issues they think are important. All issues that either side thinks are important are used and put together in various combinations to be judged. In the strike situation under study, these issues made up different *possible* contracts between management and labor. Each underlying issue—for example, *percent* of salary increase or *number* of strikers to be rehired—is in some amount on every contract. Therefore, one contract might include a 7 percent salary increase and an agreement to rehire all strikers, while another might include a 9 percent increase but only half the workers. Each person involved judged the acceptability of each contract.

When applying the conflict reduction technique, the psychologist uses statistical methods to determine three aspects of each person's *judgment policy:* (a) *weights*—that is, how important an issue is in comparison to other issues in the contract, (b) *type*—that is, whether the person views high amounts of an issue in a positive or negative way (Is a 9 percent increase better or worse for management? for labor?), and (c) the *consistency* with which the person applies the policy used. Let's work through an example.

Suppose that a father has promised to buy his teenager a car for graduation. Graduation is approaching, and they are kidding each other about *specific* cars. The father mentions a Chevette; the son shows him a Rolls Royce ad. The father mentions a VW; the son, an Impala with everything on it. Both see a need for the son to have a car (just as management and labor see a need for a new contract). Their preferences, once they get serious, might be analyzed in terms of several *issues:* price, horsepower, impact on other teenagers (especially of the opposite sex), gas mileage, and so forth. The father's judgment may be largely determined by price, and to a lesser degree, by horsepower. Gas mileage is of no concern (since the son will have to buy his own gas), and he has not even thought of impact on other teenagers. Thus he *weights* price heaviest and horsepower second but gives no weight to impact or gas mileage. The son, on the other hand, is concerned about price and impact—the more impact the better! He wants lots of horsepower but feels it's a relatively minor issue; and since he's never had to buy gas, he doesn't even think about gas mileage. He gives a lot of weight to price and impact, some weight to horsepower, and none to gas mileage.

Now what about the *types* of relationships in a person's judgment policy? The father and son most likely disagree strongly about the types of relationships—that is, about whether a high level of something is good or bad. (We have a situation here that is similar to labor negotiations in that management would be expected to view a 7 percent raise as better than a 9 percent raise, and labor would be expected to view a 9 percent raise as much more desirable than a 7 percent raise.)

The father considers price *negatively*, the *lower* the price the more he likes it. He would also rate horsepower negatively (low horsepower—good, moderate horsepower—ok, high horsepower—bad). The son's "typing" of price is not that straightforward—low-priced cars are not good, but if a car is too high priced, that's not good either; he'd prefer a moderately priced car. It doesn't follow a neat pattern. He would rate horsepower *positively*, that is, the more horsepower the better he likes it. Impact is also positively evaluated, of course.

If the issue has no importance (no weight) such as gas mileage, then the question of type does not arise; it is neither positive nor negative. It just doesn't count.

Consistency of judgment is probably clear enough. You can well imagine that the father might say price is most important on Monday, but then he sees an accident that occurred with a souped-up car reported in the paper, and on Friday he feels horsepower is the most important issue. That would be *inconsistent*. People are often inconsistent in their actual decisions, as well as in their statements about what is important. This inconsistency may cause significant problems in resolving conflicts.

The term *judgment policy* refers to the weights and types of relationships a person has for the issues when making a decision. In this example, the decision or judgment refers to the acceptability of particular *cars*. The son's policy refers to how he puts together the issues in his head, and his weights and types *describe* that policy. The father's policy is how *he* puts the issues together. His weights and types describe his policy. A psychologist with a set of judgments on real cars might have difficulty telling which issues were really influencing the judgments (the issues are all tangled together; for example, expensive cars usually have high horsepower). However, suppose we make up values for the issues so that the issues are disentangled; then we can get judgments on hypothetical cars and tell what issues are influencing the judgments.

If we could use such a set of judgments on the labor-management contracts in the strike situation to discover the negotiators' judgment policies, we could help these people understand better their own minds. That, in turn, would help communication among the negotiators. The analysis of the decisions also helps us provide an aid to help overcome inconsistency in thinking. If we can help people know better their own judgment policies, then we should be able to help people in conflict.

The actual study. Discussions were held among the six negotiators. All agreed that there were four key issues: (1) number of years the contract would run, (2) percentage of wage increase, (3) number of machine operators to be employed, and (4) number of strikers who would be recalled when the strike was settled. A number of possible contracts had to be made up and evaluated by each of the negotiators. To determine the judgment policy of the negotiators, each of the issues had to vary over the reasonable possibilities for that issue. To do that, numbers were attached to each issue, ranging from the lowest reasonable amount to the highest reasonable amount. Within that range, there were five distinct amounts for each issue. Figure 2 on the next page should make the idea of a contract clearer. Notice how the values for each issue differ between these two sample contracts.

A large number of different contracts were possible. Of these, twenty-five were selected for the negotiators to judge. These twenty-five were selected so that the full ranges of the four issues were adequately represented. Each negotiator was asked to rate each of the twenty-five total contracts on a 7-point scale, with 1 being "recommend rejection of the contract" and 7 being "recommend acceptance of the contract." Note that each negotiator looked at the values assigned each of the issues but made *a single rating* on each contract.

Some definitions and controls.   Seeing the conflict in the environment was easy enough: there had been no contract signed, and there was a long strike. But how could psychologists help to resolve the conflict? Could they reduce the problem to a question answerable by research? In the experiment, *conflict* and *conflict reduction* were defined in a precise, quantitative way by measuring agreement on the twenty-five contracts. Conflict was directly indicated by union and management disagreement on the contracts. Conflict reduction was indicated by an increase in agreement.

Note that the behavior the psychologists were observing was highly objective; if the negotiator rated a contract a 5 any observer would agree that the negotiator's rating was a 5. Using the 7-point scale not only objectified the negotiator's evaluation but also allowed the psychologist to quantify key aspects of the judgment policy.

All negotiators rated the same contracts on the same form in the same order on the same 7-point scale. An especially important form of experimental control was introduced by disentangling the issues on the contracts (that is, making them uncorrelated), since this allowed the psychologist to tell which issues were influencing the judgments.

First round of judgments.   The six negotiators were divided into three pairs, each with one management and one union representative. (Members of a given pair will be called each other's counterparts.) The conflict reduction technique was used with two pairs, but not with the third. This third pair was a control group, since the effects of the conflict reduction technique would be evaluated by comparing it with the first two (experimental) pairs. It is stretching the term *control group* to call only a single pair a control group, but when investigators step outside the laboratory and use on-the-job subjects, they do the best they can.

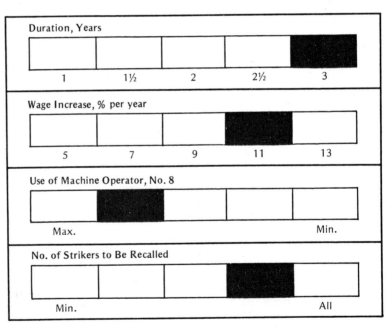

Figure 2. Two sample contracts.

These are essentially what the negotiators saw in the study. Each issue has a value on each contract. Note that "disentanglement," or zero correlation among the issues, means, for example, that a high percentage wage increase is just as likely to be a 1-year, 2-year, or 3-year contract. You cannot predict one issue from another. This is *un*like our example of the cars, where, for example, high-priced cars *tend* to have more horsepower and more impact.

The following specific steps were taken. First, each negotiator rated each contract on the 7-point scale. Next, each negotiator went through the contracts again, rating them as he *thought* his counterpart would. Each negotiator also wrote down the percentage of importance he himself felt he placed on each of the four issues after completing all the contracts. These percentages provided a *subjective importance weighting* that showed how the negotiator would *say* what he *thought* was important in his judgments.

The negotiators' judgments were then analyzed by computer to determine the policies. Each negotiator's subjective description of his own policy could then be compared with the policy computed statistically from his judgments on the contracts. (What he said could then be compared with what he did!) In addition, each member of a pair could be compared with the other to see the extent to which management and labor representatives *agreed* in their policies. Each negotiator's policy could be compared with what his counterpart thought it would be. Management negotiators' policies could be compared with each other to see if the management team presented a united front. The same could be done for the labor team.

Second round of judgments—feedback. The negotiators were shown a computer analysis of their own judgment policies. Two pairs of negotiators were shown a comparison of subject percentages they assigned with the weights the computer extracted from their first set of twenty-five judgments. They then rated all the contracts again on the 7-point scale. Each member of each experimental pair was then shown the weights and graphs *of his counterpart* and predicted his counterpart's judgments on each contract again.

The pair of control negotiators did not get this feedback. They did reevaluate the contracts and talk to each other about the issues in the way they normally would. Then they predicted each other's judgments.

The final round—negotiations. Each of the three pairs got together once again and negotiated. That is, each pair of negotiators tried to come to agreement on a common rating for each of the twenty-five contracts. What were the results of the study?

How well did the negotiators understand their own policies? Before feedback, the negotiators did not have good understanding. This showed up in several ways. At the beginning of the study, the six negotiators all agreed that four issues were crucial. Yet in their ratings of the contracts, the management negotiators' judgments were determined almost completely by the percentage of salary increase. The union negotiators' judgments were determined almost exclusively by the percentage of strikers to be recalled. When the subjective percentages were compared to the weights gotten from the computer, they did not correspond well at all.

How well did the negotiators understand each other? This question is answered by looking at the relationship before feedback between a negotiator's judgments and the predictions of his judgments by his counterpart. They were completely off base in predicting what each other thought was important. In spite of the experience each had had with the other during the actual strike, the negotiators did not understand each other!

Did the teams agree among themselves? The responses to the contracts by the three union men were compared with one another, and the responses by the management negotiators were compared with one another. The three union negotiators were similar to each other —what one liked, the other two liked. In a real negotiation, they would have been virtually interchangeable with respect to their judgments on specific contracts. But the picture was different on the other side. The three management negotiators had different policies. You could not predict what one would say about a contract from what another would say. For one of them, the shorter a contract was, the better he liked it. The other two preferred the longer contracts. On the evaluations of the wage issue, two negotiators preferred a moderate increase; for the third, the lower the increase the better he liked it. Such disagreement among negotiators, especially when they themselves are unaware of it, would obviously create havoc in any actual bargaining situation.

How consistent was each individual negotiator? How well did each negotiator agree with himself from one time to another? Not well. The three union negotiators were consistent during the first round, but became somewhat less so in the subsequent rounds. The management people were not consistent at all. It is likely they would not have been trusted by their counterparts, as they seemed to "change their mind" from contract to contract. In actuality, they were just inconsistent.

What happened to the conflict? All three pairs of negotiators began in a high degree of conflict. That is, the contracts management rated acceptable, labor tended to rate as unacceptable, and vice versa. By the end of the experiment, the two pairs who had been given feedback were in substantial agreement on their ratings of the contracts. The third pair, which had relied on traditional negotiating methods, was still in disagreement and actually had a negative relationship between their evaluations of the contracts.

We know that people have limitations on their abilities to think and communicate. We believe that their limitations often breed conflict and distrust, where conflict and distrust need not exist. The results of this experiment are relevant to the question, What can psychologists do to help? This research shows that we are developing means for reducing interpersonal conflicts. While the study described was really a demonstration, this conflict reduction method is beginning to see some use in the "real world." The techniques, as we outlined them, have been applied to the development of a land-use policy in Boulder, Colorado, the resolution of school-board conflicts, the resolution of a serious controversy in a large city about the kind of bullets the police should carry, and the resolution of conflicts in areas as diverse as water resource planning, nuclear safeguards policies, and corporate policymaking.

CAN FEAR BE REDUCED?—A LABORATORY STUDY

e all fear some objects or situations. In terms of this book, these objects are stressful. For example, many people have an aversion to animals like snakes and spiders, and many feel anxiety when boarding an airplane. Many students get "butterflies" when entering a classroom to take a big examination. These fears do not usually disrupt people's lives. But sometimes they do. Think how limited your life would be if you had such an intense fear of cars that you could not even sit in one, or how restricted your life would be if you were so terrified of crowds that you could not enter a room in which more than ten or fifteen people were gathered. Imagine the inconveniences if you lived in a large city and were so fearful of elevators that you could not bear to ride in one.

It is hard for us to understand the terror some people experience when they face such seemingly simple, everyday activities. However, some people do have specific fears that are so intense that their lives are affected. They are suffering from *phobias*. Phobic behavior is just one of the many ways that personality changes for the worse under stress. In this instance the stress is the presence of some feared object or situation. The change is the terror in the presence of the object or situation and the extremes of behavior to which people will go in order to avoid the stress.

Many methods, such as hypnosis, psychoanalysis, and tranquilizing drugs, have been used to try to help people with phobias. Recently, another technique called *systematic desensitization* has been developed to treat phobias. Systematic desensitization is based upon *classical conditioning*, originally developed by Pavlov in his experiments with dogs. Over the years people have applied classical conditioning concepts as ways of explaining the development of human behavior. While there are many theories of what causes phobias, some psychologists and psychiatrists believe that phobias have been learned by classical conditioning. They believe that phobias can also be eliminated by applying classical conditioning procedures as therapeutic techniques. This is where systematic desensitization comes in.

Systematic desensitization sets up conditions whereby the person repeatedly "encounters" the feared object or situation while in a relaxed state. Relaxation and fear, it is argued, just cannot go together, and the terror is essentially "conditioned out." The relaxation blocks the fear, and the person is conditioned not to be afraid. But how is this accomplished? How can someone be in the presence of something that terrifies him or her and at the same time be relaxed? We will go through the steps a psychologist might take in desensitizing a person who has a phobia.

Suppose, for example, a young man comes to a psychologist with the complaint that he is terrified of riding in automobiles and has been unable to go anywhere not within walking distance for six months. First, a psychological examination is conducted, involving an interview and perhaps some psychological tests. This is done to determine what the problem is and whether systematic desensitization is likely to be the best treatment.

If systematic desensitization is considered appropriate, the first step is to train the young man in "deep muscle relaxation" by spending a few sessions specifically teaching him how to tense and relax various muscles in his body, and how to practice this relaxation at home. Once he is able to attain a good state of muscle relaxation, the difficult job of training him to stay relaxed in the presence of the feared object begins. This is done by using a *fear hierarchy* together with *visual imagery.*

The patient is asked to make up a list of specific situations related to his fear. Some items on the list might be (1) being forced into a car and driven at breakneck speed through traffic, (2) approaching a parked car and putting his hand on the door handle, and (3) being told he has to ride in a car to the store. Then the patient and psychologist discuss each "scene" and put the items in order, beginning with what the person reports to be the least fear provoking and ending with the most terrifying. This list is called the fear hierarchy.

Once the hierarchy is established and relaxation training completed, desensitization begins. The patient relaxes himself. Then in a calm, quiet, and reassuring voice, the psychologist asks him to imagine vividly the *least* frightening scene in his hierarchy. As soon as the patient does this without feeling any fear, he is told to stop imagining the scene, to continue relaxing, and then to imagine the next scene on the list. If at any time during the process he feels fearful, the patient signals this fear by slightly raising an index finger. This small, relatively effortless response is used so that the patient's state of relaxation is minimally disrupted. Whenever he raises his finger, he is told to stop imagining, to re-relax, and then re-imagine the last item on the list that produced no fear. This process continues until the patient can remain relaxed while vividly imagining what was originally the most terrifying scene on the list.

The patient might also be asked to engage in some desensitization outside of the clinical setting. That is, as treatment progresses, the psychologist might have the patient do some "homework," like walking around used car lots or sitting in a parked car. Once the hierarchy is completed, the patient might be instructed to go for a short ride if he hasn't already done so.

If all goes well, the automobile phobia is conquered by the time the hierarchy is completed (in reality a number of different hierarchies might be needed); and the patient can now ride in cars, even though he might still feel somewhat tense.

Numerous clinical case reports follow the above procedure. However, many questions exist concerning systematic desensitization; for example, How long lasting are the treatment effects? Is systematic desensitization any more effective than other, older approaches? Is the effectiveness of systematic desensitization primarily due to patients' *expectancies* that they will improve rather than to the method itself? These and other questions are targets of research. In order to show how some psychologists have addressed the question, Is systematic desensitization an effective treatment, and if so, why? let us review a well-known experiment (Davidson, 1968). Davidson was interested in not only how well treatment works but also whether it is possible to help people without combining deep muscle relaxation with visual imagery of scenes related to their fears.

We have seen that before carrying out a project, researchers must go through a number of steps that provide the definitions and operations for the experiment. Let's recreate the steps involved in Davidson's study.

We can first ask, Is systematic desensitization an effective treatment for phobias? At the simplest level this requires one comparison, a comparison between phobic patients who received systematic desensitization therapy and phobic controls who received no therapy. If the treated group improves and the untreated group stays the same or gets worse, then we might conclude that systematic desensitization (or some component of this complex procedure) is a useful treatment for phobias. Since Davidson wanted to demonstrate that systematic desensitization "works," he included these two groups. But, as we said, he was also interested in whether or not success depends upon having people imagine increasingly fearful scenes relevant to their phobia while they are relaxed. So he needed two more groups. One group was in a state of relaxation while they imagined scenes *not relevant* to their fear; the other group was *not* in a state of relaxation while they imagined scenes *relevant* to their fear.

Davidson compared how much improvement occurred among these four groups: (1) systematic desensitization, (2) relaxation without imagery of relevant scenes, (3) imagery of relevant scenes without relaxation, and (4) no treatment. From these comparisons, Davidson could answer—for his specific experiment—the two questions, Does systematic desensitization work? and Is it necessary to pair relaxation with relevant, fearful images in order to reduce fear? These four groups represent Davidson's experimental design. Now let's examine the procedure more specifically.

Davidson's subjects were female college students who were fearful of nonpoisonous snakes. He first asked a class of introductory psychology students for volunteers who had such fears to participate in an experiment on how psychologists might remove common anxieties. He then tested their degree of fearfulness by bringing each one into a room containing a harmless snake in a glass cage and having the subject go through a *behavioral approach test*. This test had thirteen steps, each more fear-producing than the previous (e.g., placing a gloved hand on the glass near the snake, touching the snake with the gloved hand, and finally holding the snake barehanded for 30 seconds). Subjects were asked to complete as many of these steps as they could. As each step was completed, each student rated her fear on a scale from 1 to 10. Any subject who touched the snake barehanded was not considered fearful enough and was excluded from the study.

The results of the behavioral approach test did four things for Davidson: (1) It provided objective measurement of what he meant by "fearful," (i.e., the number of approach steps a subject could complete and a self-rating of the intensity of felt fears). (2) It gave him a way of dropping subjects who did not fear snakes. This is an important experimental control. (3) It provided a basis for objective evaluation of the effectiveness of treatment. He could define "getting better" in two ways: by comparing the number of approach steps completed before and after treatment and by comparing changes in the fear ratings. (4) It allowed him to equate the groups on fearfulness—a highly desirable form of experimental control.

Once subjects were selected, they were assigned to one of the four groups. Davidson used the behavioral approach test results to ensure that each group contained equally fearful subjects. Thus any differences between the groups after treatment could not be attributed to differences that had existed before treatment.

At this point, you should be asking yourself questions like, What scenes did the experimenter use to make up the hierarchy relevant to snake fears? What scenes were used for subjects in the group that imagined items unrelated to fear of snakes? How long was each treatment session? How many sessions were there? How was relaxation training carried out? What experiences did the no-treatment group receive? All of these questions must be answered before we have a good picture of the experiment. Let's go through each group and see what was done.

Systematic desensitization group. In the first session subjects were taught to relax. This was done by using a 30-minute tape recording instructing the students how and when to "tense and relax" their muscles, and giving them suggestions like "you feel heavy" and "you feel calm." In the second session the group constructed the fear hierarchy by ranking 26 statements describing scenes about snakes in order of how frightening each scene was. Then, the entire systematic desensitization procedure was carried out. That is, the scenes were systematically presented while subjects were relaxed. There were a maximum of nine 45-minute sessions, during which all subjects completed the hierarchy. Each subject then went through the behavioral approach test, exactly as before.

Relaxation with irrelevant imagery. These subjects received the same relaxation training as did subjects in the systematic desensitization group. They also ranked twenty-six scenes, but these were *not* related to snakes or fear of snakes (for example, You are about six and your family is discussing at the dinner table where to go for a ride on Sunday afternoon). Then the experimenter relaxed the subjects and asked them to imagine each scene. Finally, they, too, went through the behavioral approach test a second time. Each subject was individually matched to a person in the systematic desensitization group not only on original level of fear but also on the number of sessions, length of sessions, and number and duration of each imagination experience. The same matching was done for the next two groups.

Relevant imagery—no relaxation. These subjects were asked to imagine each scene relevant to snake fears. They imagined them in the same order, for the same amount of time, and for the same number of sessions as did subjects in the systematic desensitization group. They also redid the behavioral approach test, but they received *no* relaxation training.

No treatment. The subjects in this group went through the behavioral approach test as did all other subjects; they repeated this test once treatment sessions were completed in the other three groups.

We can summarize this experimental design in a table that shows how the control groups nicely separate the components of systematic desensitization.

RELEVANT IMAGERY

		YES	NO
RELAXATION	YES	Systematic desensitization	Controls for possible effects of relaxation alone
	NO	Controls for possible effects of imagery alone	Controls for possible effects of being in the experiment and expecting to get better

What were the findings? In terms of the differences in steps completed in the pretreatment to posttreatment behavior approach tests, the outcome was very clear. Only the systematic desensitization group improved; that is, they came closer to the snake after treatment than they had in the original approach test. In addition, subjects who improved showed the greatest decreases in self-rated feelings of fear during the posttreatment test.

What do these findings mean in terms of our question regarding the effects of systematic desensitization? Clearly, the systematic desensitization operations led to significant changes in behavior where other "control" operations did not. We can argue from this particular experiment that it is necessary to combine relaxation with relevant visual imagery in order to obtain the changes.

All this is *consistent* with the statement that systematic desensitization is an effective treatment for phobias. You should note that the findings from this experimental analogue study *do not* relate in any direct way back to the question, *Why* does personality change under stress? The study does *not* address the issue of what "makes" people fearful—rather the work represents one effort to address the question, How can psychologists help? The research does not address the question, Does the treatment work "in the real world"? The following report does.

CAN FEAR BE REDUCED?—A CASE STUDY

 e have just seen that systematic desensitization is effective in reducing fear of snakes. However, remember that Davidson's research was an analogue. That is, it dealt with a phobia that was only analogous— similar in some ways—to the phobias that lead people to seek help in a clinic. The fear he studied was not highly disruptive to his subjects. It is, in fact, one that most people share. Treating it did not improve their lives. Furthermore, his subjects were not "real" patients seeking help for their phobias; instead they were students who had volunteered for a research project. They probably never would have sought help for their "difficulty."

Does systematic desensitization help people suffering from seriously disruptive phobias?

One way to answer this question might be to give systematic desensitization therapy to one group of phobic patients and to leave a matched control group untreated (at least for a time). While this general research strategy has often been used in research into a variety of emotional disorders, certain practical problems may make it unfeasible. One major difficulty is that it is hard to get a large enough group of phobic patients together at one time in one place. Even if we could get enough patients to make up two groups, it is likely that there would be such wide differences among the people that group comparisons would be virtually meaningless. For example, some patients might fear heights, others riding in cars; some might fear three or four objects, others only one; some might have been phobic for years, others for months, and still others for only days. The intensity of the fears may range from mild discomfort to terror. Such differences are critical in terms of how long treatment may take, the number of fear hierarchies needed, how long treatment effects may last, or even whether treatment will work at all. In other words, even if we could get enough phobic people to form groups for an experiment, it is highly unlikely that they would be similar enough to make meaningful comparisons among them.

Does this mean that we cannot scientifically examine our treatment operations using real patients? Our answer is an emphatic No! In fact, the psychotherapy literature has many examples of research using such "subjects." While this literature reflects a wide range of research strategies, one of the most common is the *case history report*. This approach involves a careful description of a particular patient, a particular set of therapy procedures, and specific outcomes of the treatment. While there are problems with such a research design, there are also advantages. We will discuss the advantages and disadvantages later. For now, we will illustrate how two psychologists approached the question of the effectiveness of systematic desensitization, using a person suffering from a "real-life problem."

Silverman and Geer (1968) report the case of a nineteen-year-old phobic woman. Their first step was to gather background data on the patient and the problem. They had to define the problem clearly and obtain the objective information necessary for them to evaluate the treatment and communicate their methods and results. Thus the following information was obtained. The patient initially complained of "terrifying," recurrent nightmares she had been having for approximately four years. They contained three basic themes: (1) walking across a bridge made of wooden slats high over some water, with the fear of falling through the slats, (2) walking on a path on the side of a bridge on a windy day, with the fear of being blown into the water, and (3) driving across a bridge, with the fear of falling out of her car. One or another of these dreams occurred twice or more a week.

During the course of the initial examination, it was also discovered that for as long as she could remember, she had been afraid to cross bridges. In fact she reported that she had never crossed a bridge on foot and that she would not do so under any circumstances. She also reported severe anxiety when she had to drive over a bridge. This she would do only when absolutely necessary, and even then, only if she could drive in the center lane of traffic.

She reported no fear of heights when she was in enclosed spaces, such as a room on the top floor of a tall building. However, she indicated that she would not go near a railing on a high overlook or sit high in any grandstand in which she could see through to the ground.

In terms of general adjustment, she was an honor student, was engaged to be married, and reported no other emotional problems. Given this and given the nature of her difficulties (a highly specific fear), the therapists decided that systematic desensitization would be the best approach to try. She initially complained of disturbing dreams. In fact, she came to these psychologists because she had learned of their interest in recurrent nightmares. Silverman and Geer decided they would not treat the dreams directly. They had previously treated a patient with recurrent nightmares and a related phobia by treating the phobia. They were successful—when the phobia disappeared, so did the nightmares.

Thus the psychological examination provided them with the potential for two objective measures of the effectiveness of treatment: (1) the frequency of nightmares and (2) whether or not the patient could successfully walk across a bridge.

During the first two treatment sessions, the subject was trained in deep muscle relaxation and instructed in how to visualize good images. The following 6-item fear hierarchy was constructed:

1. approaching a long, high bridge by automobile

2. driving across a bridge in the center lane

3. driving across a bridge in the outside lane

4. approaching a bridge on foot

5. crossing the footpath at the side of a bridge on a clear day

6. crossing the footpath at the side of a bridge on a windy day.

Once the hierarchy was constructed and relaxation training completed, systematic desensitization began. That is, items on the hierarchy were systematically paired with deep muscle relaxation until the scenes could be imagined without fear. By the end of seven therapy sessions, which took four weeks, the patient could imagine all the scenes on the hierarchy without expressing fear. Also, during the last two weeks of treatment she reported having had no nightmares. She had been having them regularly in previous weeks. In fact, during the last two weeks she experienced two *pleasant* dreams about crossing bridges. During the last therapy session, she volunteered that she thought that she could walk across a bridge. These facts all suggest the treatment had worked. The patient could calmly imagine scenes that previously terrified her, her nightmares had stopped, and she felt capable of crossing a bridge, something she had never done. However, the critical behavior in determining whether the treatment had been successful is not what occurs in the clinical setting but what occurs in the patient's life.

One week following treatment the therapist observed at a distance while the patient walked over a long, high bridge. She was able to stop frequently to look over the railing into the water and said later that she had not been afraid.

This seems to be strong evidence that treatment had been effective, but Silverman and Geer wanted to know if the changes were long lasting. Thus they interviewed the patient one month later. No more nightmares and no more fear! Another follow-up in six months showed the same result. No nightmares. No fears.

The treatment "worked." The nightmares were gone, and the patient could do things she could not do in the past. But how does this positive clinical outcome relate to the broader question, Is systematic desensitization effective? The data are consistent with the statement that "it works," just as Davidson's data were. But we must qualify conclusions drawn from results of this or any single case study. There were no control subjects—that is, there was no one "just like" the patient who did not receive systematic desensitization. Therefore, we cannot be certain that she would not have gotten better without any treatment. Also, we had no similar subjects who received some other, perhaps even simpler treatment (that is, a couple of counseling sessions) that may have had equally good results. While this single case study does not *prove* that the treatment works, the results are consistent with such an interpretation. In addition to lending some evidence to the usefulness of systematic desensitization, this study does something else. It provides other therapists with some evidence that the techniques may be effective for their patients who suffer similar problems, and that's very important! Thus, by combining the results of single case studies with other research findings (e.g., other case studies finding similar results or other research suggesting that alternative methods, such as a couple of counseling sessions, *won't* help), the psychologist can be guided toward treatment that has a good chance of helping. Remember that Silverman and Geer decided to take the present treatment approach with this patient because of previous success with a similar problem. Other therapists combining the case reports on these two patients with other research data are now better prepared to help people suffering from terrifying dreams and related phobias. The study speaks directly to the question, How can psychologists help?

We have touched on some important research issues in this section, issues that relate to the generality of the case study data and the usefulness of this particular basic strategy of research. The case study has been criticized on these issues, but the issues are much more general, and we will return to them later.

CAN BIOFEEDBACK ELIMINATE HEADACHES?

ne of the most frequent effects of stress is the common tension headache. Everyone is familiar with the television representations of this very unpleasant experience—hammers striking anvils in our heads, drums beating to throbbing rhythms between our ears. Most people suffer headaches occasionally, but some have tension headaches so frequently that their lives are seriously disrupted. Thus there has been considerable interest in finding ways to help prevent their occurrence.

The causes of headaches range from hangovers to brain tumors. However, it has been pretty well established that the specific pain called *tension headache* is associated with continued contractions of the muscles in the scalp and neck. That is, for some people stress seems to cause specific muscle groups to contract, and this constant contraction leads to a headache. Thus psychologists asked the question, If we can teach people to relax these specific muscles can we alleviate their tension headaches?

We have already seen that deep muscle relaxation is used effectively in systematic desensitization therapy. You will recall that this relaxation is accomplished by talking the patient through a series of tensing and relaxing exercises. Another way of teaching the deep relaxation of a specific muscle group is called *biofeedback*. In biofeedback people receive direct information regarding certain aspects of their biological states. People can be "wired up" so they can see a signal light go on if their heart rate increases or so they can hear a tone increase or decrease in intensity as their breathing rate increases or decreases. They can also be given direct information regarding how tense a set of muscles is at any given time. It is this biofeedback—in this case, information about muscle activity—that psychologists can use to help people with tension headaches. Let's explore some research on the effectiveness of biofeedback in alleviating tension headaches.

Budzynski, Stoyva, and Adler (1969) carried out a series of five single case studies in which biofeedback was applied to patients with tension headaches. All the patients improved. However, as we have seen, the single case study (or even a series of such studies) has limitations. The major one is that there are no control subjects, making it difficult to know which aspect of the treatment operations is effective, or if improvement would have occurred without treatment.

Thus Budzynski, Stoyva, Adler, and Mullaney (1973) decided they would expand upon the above case study research with a formal experiment. First, it was necessary to obtain a large enough group of people with tension headaches to make it possible to do the research. As we saw in the last section, obtaining large enough samples of people suffering from some emotional problems can be extremely difficult. However, tension headaches are much more common than phobias, and tension headache problems tend to be much more similar to one another than are phobias. Remember that patients must be highly similar on important dimensions. Let's see how these researchers went about doing this.

The first step was to advertise in a local newspaper, asking people who suffered from tension headaches to volunteer for a research project at the university college of medicine. People who called were screened over the telephone so that the researchers could immediately rule out those whose headaches were clearly due to sources other than muscular contraction. Volunteers who passed this initial screening were given medical and psychiatric examinations to make sure that they suffered tension headaches and to rule out other organic or psychiatric problems. This screening ensured that the patients for the research would be comparable at least on one important dimension, the specific nature of the disorder to be treated. But how about the frequency and intensity of their headaches? These had to be equal in the groups to be formed. The next step in the selection process was aimed at solving this problem.

Following the medical-psychiatric examination, the prospective subjects were asked to keep records of their headaches. During each waking hour for the next two weeks they made a rating on the following 0 to 5 scale.

5—intense, incapacitating pain

4—severe headache that made concentration difficult but allowed the patient to do nondemanding tasks

3—painful headache but one that did not interfere with the patient's work

2—intensity of pain that could be ignored at times

1—low-level headache of which the patient wasn't much aware unless he really attended to it

0—no headache was present at the time of the rating

For each subject, the researchers averaged the numbers obtained from the hourly ratings for each week. This provided a somewhat rough but quantitative measure of headache activity. This headache score was used in two ways. First, it allowed the researchers to make sure all patients in this study were experiencing at least a moderate level of headache. That is, patients were not kept in the experiment if their scores did not reach a certain point. This headache score also provided an objective measure of pretreatment headache activity for comparison with posttreatment headache activity. Thus these pretreatment ratings represented a *baseline* of the behavior of interest. Also, during this two-week period the researchers measured each subject's muscle activity (EMG) in the forehead. This measure, a pen-tracing of electrical activity in the muscles looks like a polygraph or a "lie-detector" record. This provided another objective baseline measure of tension that could be compared with EMG activity during and after treatment.

The researchers engaged in one more selection operation. All remaining subjects were given a standard personality test. Anyone who appeared to have marked psychological problems (aside from tension headaches) was dropped from the study. Thus the authors used a four-stage screening process in an effort to obtain subjects who were comparable on as many important dimensions as possible. At the completion of subject selection eighteen patients remained, sixteen of whom were female. The age range was twenty-two to forty-four, and the subjects included secretaries, housewives, teachers, graduate students, nurses, and a writer. Volunteers who were dropped from the study were offered treatment for their headaches, but they were not included in the experiment.

It was then necessary to form the appropriate experimental and control groups. From your previous reading it should be obvious that one group has to receive the biofeedback treatment, while a second group of patients should receive no treatment whatsoever. A posttreatment comparison between these two groups would indicate whether or not the biofeedback therapy was better than no therapy at all. But these researchers decided to use a third group, as well. We can see why by outlining the procedures for the biofeedback therapy group. Six of the eighteen subjects were assigned at random to each of three groups. The biofeedback therapy procedures can best be described by quoting the instructions given to the six patients assigned to this group. They were each told the following:

Tension headaches are primarily due to sustained contraction or tightness in the muscles of the scalp and neck.

The goal of this study is to learn to relax your muscles so that the tension level never gets too high, and you no longer get headaches. This will involve a great deal of work on your part, both here in the lab, and also at home.

In order to help you learn, we are going to provide you with information as to the level of muscle tension in your forehead region. You will hear a series of clicks in the headphones. The click rate will be proportional to your forehead tension; that is, the higher the tension, the faster the click rate. Your job will be to find out what makes the click rate slow down, because this means lower

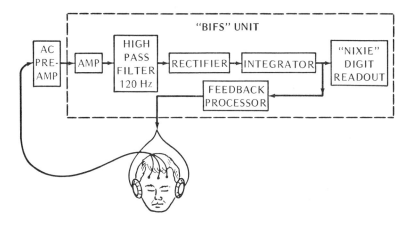

Figure 3. Functional diagram of the EMG feedback system.

muscle tension. Try to eliminate those things that make the click rate go faster. Do not try too hard, or this will defeat your goal of deep relaxation. Remember to keep your attention focused on the clicks—do not let your mind wander.
This session will last about 30 minutes.
Remember—do not go to sleep.
Any questions? (Budzynski et al., 1973, pp. 487–88)

The "wiring" does *not* mean that subjects received electric shocks. The apparatus shown in Figure 3 *picks up* electrical activity from the subject's muscles, records the activity, and translates it to clicks that are delivered back to the subject. For sixteen sessions (usually two per week) individual subjects were wired to the feedback apparatus, with the electrodes placed right over the muscles of their foreheads. As you can see from the instructions, their task was to learn how to relax their forehead muscles by using the signals coming directly from these muscles, signals that told them whether or not they were relaxing properly. Subjects were also asked to practice relaxing at home without the feedback for 15-20 minutes per day.

If the biofeedback group had been compared only to a no-treatment control group, it would be difficult to know what aspects of the "treatment package" had produced any observed changes. For example, we would not know if changes in headache activity were due to being told to relax, to having sixteen sessions with a psychologist, to practicing relaxation at home, to hearing a series of "clicks" that "took one's mind off one's problems," or what. We certainly wouldn't know if it was the feedback per se that was the important component. These potential sources of change had to be controlled. In order to achieve this control, six subjects in a "pseudofeedback" group received the following instructions.

Tension headaches are primarily due to sustained contraction or tightness in the muscles of the scalp and neck.
The goal of this study is to learn to relax your muscles so that the tension level

never gets too high, and you no longer get headaches. This will involve a great deal of work on your part, both here in the lab, and also at home.

As you relax, it is important to keep out intruding thoughts. The varying click rate you will hear in the headphones will help you to keep out these thoughts. It is very important to keep your attention focused on the varying rate of clicks. Do not let your mind wander.

This session will last about 30 minutes.

Remember—do not go to sleep.

Any questions? (Budzynski et al., 1973, p. 488)

The number of clicks presented to this "pseudofeedback" group was exactly the same as that given to the therapy group. This was done by playing tape recordings of the clicks from real feedback sessions into the earphones of these subjects. The difference was that clicks heard by the pseudofeedback control group were unrelated to the state of their forehead muscles—that is, the clicks *did not* constitute biofeedback. Subjects in this group were also told to do the home relaxation practice.

Throughout the sixteen sessions two objective measures were obtained for each subject in the therapy and pseudotherapy groups: (1) the forehead muscle tension (EMG) levels during the session and (2) the continual hourly ratings on headache activity. The no-treatment control subjects simply continued to do the hourly ratings; they got no other instructions, no wiring to the apparatus, nothing else. Once the experiment was completed, all control subjects were offered biofeedback therapy for their headaches.

How did it all come out? If biofeedback worked, we would expect the muscle tension levels to drop in the therapy group. That is, over the sessions these subjects should show less tension in their forehead muscles than they did during the baseline measurement. Also, these subjects should show a greater decrease in muscular tension over the sixteen sessions than the pseudofeedback controls. This is exactly what was found.

But what about headache activity? Again, what we would expect is a drop in the ratings of headache severity in the biofeedback therapy group and little or no change in hourly ratings of headache severity in either of the control groups. This is precisely what occurred. There was no appreciable change in headache activity among control subjects. To investigate the lasting effects of the treatment, the investigators obtained ratings of headache activity for three months following completion of the biofeedback. Subjects from the therapy group *continued to improve*. Also, muscular tension measured at the end of the follow-up period remained high in the pseudotherapy group while the treated subjects showed about the same lowered levels of tension as they showed immediately after the sixteen training sessions. A considerable amount of additional follow-up data was gathered for up to eighteen months after treatment, all of which was consistent with the initial finding that biofeedback therapy was helpful.

The results from this research are encouraging, but this is not the end of the story—not by a long shot. A number of questions remain. For example, would the same or better results be obtained by using deep muscle relaxation exercises without the biofeedback procedures? Patients might improve as much or more if they were talked through the relaxation of the specific muscles involved much in the same way as is done in systematic desensitization. How would biofeedback treatment compare with approaches to treating tension other than those involving muscle relaxation (for example, psychotherapy aimed at discovering the psychological sources of the tension and at teaching patients to deal more effectively with those stimuli)?

Another whole area of research relates to improving the biofeedback approach itself. Budzynski and his colleagues are engaged in this now. They are asking questions like, How can the home relaxation component of the treatment be improved? In this vein they are experimenting with relaxation tape recordings and portable biofeedback equipment that the patient can use at home. While many questions need to be answered, it seems fair at this point to agree with these researchers that "even though (biofeedback) training alone is not effective in all cases, the technique would seem to be of considerable value for a substantial proportion of tension headache cases" (Budzynski et al., 1973, p. 495). Thus, given a patient with a specific kind of tension headache, the biofeedback therapy package represents one way in which psychologists may be able to help.

DOES CHANGING THE ENVIRONMENT CHANGE THE BEHAVIOR?

n the previous section on biofeedback treatment of tension headaches, you might have noticed that the psychologists were not interested in *why* the patients suffered from headaches. It was important to know that the pain was due to muscular tension, but the psychologists never asked the question, What are the psychological sources of that tension? Some of the patients may have suffered from tension headaches because of intense anger that they could not express openly. Others may have been experiencing problems at work or school, while still others may have experienced serious psychological traumas in childhood. However, the investigators considered such explanations to be irrelevant to the decision of whether to use biofeedback as a treatment.

We are going to examine another way psychologists try to help, a way that *totally ignores* the question of what is causing the behavior, at least as cause is usually understood. Some psychologists are not concerned with causal explanations, such as emotional states, poor interpersonal relationships, traumatic childhood experiences, and so forth. They regard such explanations as premature in psychology. Instead, they are concerned with what *observable* events in the environment regularly occur *immediately* before and *immediately* after a specific behavior. They want to know if and how a particular act is rewarded, if and how it is punished, and what *signals* provide information about whether the act will be punished or rewarded. The basic idea behind this approach is that specific events immediately following a specific behavior may reinforce that behavior and that this reinforcement makes it more likely that the behavior will occur again in the same situation. Thus the question of how psychologists might help is reduced to the question, Can behavior be changed by changing the immediate consequences of that behavior?

The example we will discuss is a case history of the treatment of a severely disturbed 3½-year-old boy named Dicky (Wolf, Risley, & Mees, 1964). The investigators applied principles developed in the laboratory to Dicky's self-destructive behavior.

Dicky appeared to be a normal child until he was nine months old; then it was discovered that he had cataracts in both eyes. At about this time he began having trouble going to sleep and also began to display unusual temper tantrums. In his second year of life he had a series of eye operations, resulting in the removal of the lenses of both eyes. This meant that in order for him to see normally, he would have to wear eyeglasses. He refused. His parents tried for a year both to get him to wear glasses and to cope with his violent temper tantrums. They failed. Some idea of the severity of Dicky's behavior is given in the following quotation.

Dicky did not eat normally and lacked normal social and verbal repertoires. His tantrums included self-destructive behaviors such as head-banging, face-slapping, hair-pulling, and face-scratching. His mother reported that after a severe tantrum "he was a mess, all black and blue and bleeding." He would not sleep at night, forcing one or both parents to remain by his bed. Sedatives, tranquilizers, and restraints were tried, without success (pp. 305–6).

Dicky's parents took him to a variety of specialists and got a variety of diagnoses. Finally, when he was three, they had him admitted to a mental hospital where his condition was diagnosed as childhood schizophrenia, an extremely serious condition that is difficult to treat effectively. He was released in three months with the report that there had been some improvement. However, he still would not wear glasses. Dicky's ophthalmologist now told the parents that unless he began to wear glasses within six months, he would become virtually blind—permanently.

At this point, Wolf, Risley, and Mees were asked to try to train Dicky to wear glasses. They began by observing a 20-minute interaction between Dicky and his mother, and saw a 20-minute temper tantrum. They recommended that Dicky be readmitted to the hospital so that he would be separated from his mother while they tried to reduce the undesired behavior and train him to wear glasses.

Wolf, Risley, and Mees did not work with Dicky directly. They worked with the ward attendants and with the parents, giving them careful instructions about how to treat Dicky and about what behaviors and environmental events to record. Detailed, accurate record-keeping is absolutely necessary for this treatment. Remember that this treatment approach assumes that the *consequences* of a specific behavior strongly determine whether or not that behavior will be repeated. To change behavior by manipulating its consequences (systematically rewarding and punishing it), we must have detailed records of the responses, the manipulations (rewards and punishments), and any other events that may be influencing that behavior. Otherwise, we would not know how to adjust manipulations that may not be working. Nor would we know what specific manipulations had led to what specific behavior changes.

Wolf, Risley, and Mees decided to deal with several aspects of Dicky's behavior concurrently. They attempted to reduce his tantrums and his sleeping and eating problems, to teach Dicky to keep his glasses on—not to throw them—and to establish appropriate verbal and social behavior. Let's examine two of these closely.

Temper tantrums. Dicky's temper tantrums were violent and self-destructive. Under normal circumstances, the consequences of temper tantrums are unpredictable. Parents are often quite perplexed and threatened by this behavior and respond to it by ignoring, punishing, or cuddling the child, depending on their mood, the circumstances of the tantrum, and other factors that may be unknown to the child. In fact, it is a kind of standard scene in situation television comedies.

1. Child throws tantrum
2. Mother scolds and fusses at child
3. Child continues
4. Mother threatens to tell Father
5. Father enters, Mother demands he spank child
6. Father spanks
7. Mother scolds Father
8. Mother loves and cuddles child

If the consequences of behavior are significant determinants of future behavior, what systematic effects can possibly occur if the consequences are, so far as the child can determine, so unpredictable?

Wolf, Risley, and Mees made sure the consequences of Dicky's tantrums were predictable. Every time he threw a tantrum, he was placed in his room, and his door was closed until the tantrum stopped. In order to collect the data needed, and also to communicate clearly with the ward attendants and parents, a temper tantrum was defined objectively. A tantrum was the simultaneous occurrence of two or more of the following three behaviors: whining, crying, or face-slapping. A severe tantrum was defined as involving more seriously self-destructive behaviors: head-banging, hair-pulling, or face-scratching. The mild punishment of putting Dicky in his room involved some rewarding aspects, such as the social contact and individual attention he got briefly from the attendant. However, it removed the possibility of continuous attention during the tantrum. It also allowed the therapists to reward nontantrum behavior by opening the door when the tantrum stopped. As time passed, Dicky's parents were permitted to visit him, and he began making trips home. These events, summarized below, are marked on Figure 4 on page 85, which presents the data for severe tantrums.

At (a) Dicky's parents were permitted their first one-hour visit. Subsequently they made several scheduled visits a week, during which an attendant observed and instructed them in their behavior with Dicky.

At (b) the father put Dicky to bed on the ward for the first time.

At (c) Dicky began wearing his glasses.

At (d) the mother put Dicky to bed on the ward for the first time.

Midway between (d) and (e) Dicky began short home visits accompanied by the attendant.

At (e) Dicky spent his first night at home.

At (f) Dicky spent a second night at home.

After (f) he spent an average of three nights a week at home, increasing to five nights a week during the final month. (Wolf, Risley, & Mees, 1964, p. 307)

The graph speaks volumes. Dicky's severe tantrums became progressively rarer as the behavior modification program progressed. You can see the effects of the various events, such as home visits, from the graph. It seems that Dicky's tantrums were fairly well under the control of the systematic environmental consequences arranged by the investigators.

Glasses-wearing. The problem posed here for the investigators is very different. In stressing the importance for future behavior of the consequences of behavior, we have been stressing one of the fundamental principles of reinforcement theory. An action that is rewarded, or reinforced, will tend to be repeated. But suppose you are interested in a complex response, one that rarely if ever occurs. If it is not made, how can you reinforce it? Consider the present situation. Dicky had steadfastly resisted any and all attempts at making him wear glasses. Consider what might happen if the investigators had no alternative but to wait for the desired response to occur so that they could reinforce it. Dicky would go blind. There is an alternative. It is referred to as *shaping*, or *successive approximations*. The experimenter first adopts the procedure of reinforcing anything that resembles the desired but complex response. When this first approximation to the desired response is well learned, the experimenter waits until a better response, or a closer approximation to the desired one, is made before giving reinforcement. Progressing in this way—by a skillful use of rewards—very complex chains of behavior can be shaped.

Could Dicky be shaped to wear glasses?   One attendant was selected to do the shaping. He was instructed in the procedure and spent two or three twenty-minute sessions with Dicky each day. The reward selected for use in shaping the glasses-wearing was food: Dicky was to get small bites of candy or fruit for making the right response—or, in the beginning, approximating the right response. But here a problem arises. In order for shaping to work, the reinforcement must be delivered *immediately after the desired response.* If Dicky is in the far corner of the room and he moves the glasses toward his head, you can't pop a piece of food into his mouth at just the right moment. If you walk over and give him candy, he might be smashing the glasses by the time you get there. So a means of immediately delivering the reinforcement must be developed.

There is a solution. The trick is first to take some stimulus that can be delivered from a distance and present it repeatedly just before reinforcement. In Dicky's case the procedure was to have Dicky get small bites of the candy or fruit right after the attendant made a clicking noise with a toy noisemaker. After this was done for several sessions, Dicky would go to the bowl of reinforcers whenever he heard the clicks. The click meant that food was there for the taking, so now the *click* could be used to shape behavior. The click could be delivered quickly and from any part of the room, and it had acquired reinforcing properties.

The shaping sessions began by laying several pairs of glassless frames around the room. At first Dicky was reinforced just for picking them up and holding them or carrying them. Then he was reinforced only for bringing them close to his head, then only for putting them on. Problems developed. The attendant doing the shaping could not get Dicky to put the glasses on straight. Dicky would only put them on so that the earpieces were under, rather than over, his ears and so that the eye holes did not line up with his eyes. Dicky's progress was halted.

Two reasons for the problems were possible. First, the attendant was inexperienced in the shaping process. Second, the ward staff was reluctant to deprive Dicky of food, and thus the reinforcers were relatively weak. After two weeks, Wolf, Risley, and Mees changed the procedure to deal with the second possibility. Dicky's breakfast was made contingent upon closer approximations to glasses-wearing. He would get his breakfast, a bite at a time, depending on his responses. Two more weeks passed without success, and the glasses themselves were modified with larger earpieces and a "roll-bar" going over the top of the head to keep the earpieces up over the ears. Another week passed without success, and the psychologists themselves intervened. They spent a day with the attendant and Dicky, directing the shaping procedures. They added a second bar to the glasses, this time to the back. In effect, the glasses were now put on and worn like a cap. They began the shaping at breakfast time, with bites of food again being contingent upon approximations to glasses-wearing. The breakfast session was ineffective. So Dicky got little to eat. This time, however, lunch was also used as a shaping session. Dicky's glasses-wearing behavior did not improve, so he again did not get much to eat. A third session was carried out at about two in the afternoon, and Dicky was very hungry. He was particularly interested in the ice cream that the three psychologists happened to have brought with them. The deprivation had greatly increased the power of the reinforcers, and now the investigators elected to use the prescription lenses rather than the empty frames. There was a great deal of behavior like the right behavior, and the investigators had a relatively easy time picking out better and better approximations. At the end of thirty minutes of shaping they had reinforced both the putting on and looking through the glasses sufficiently so that they could show Dicky interesting objects, with the hope of maintaining his "looking behavior." After this, progress was rapid, and he wore his glasses continuously while eating. Soon, a variety of other, less concrete reinforcers were maintaining the behavior. For example, the attendant would take Dicky for a walk if he was wearing his glasses, but the walk would be terminated if he took them off. When Dicky was released from the hospital, he was wearing his glasses for an average of twelve hours a day. The results are illustrated by Figure 5.

The research tradition represented by Wolf, Risley, and Mees sees the control of behavior as an immediately attainable goal. You have read what they did. You may have some ideas about why Dicky's behavior changed, perhaps in terms of expectancies or perhaps willpower. But note that Wolf, Risley, and Mees did not theorize. They did not think it was necessary.

If you analyze the "experiment" in terms of what has been written about the other studies, you might consider it to be deficient with respect to the use of formal experimental controls. Only one boy's data were reported, and no control group was used. However, Dicky served as his own control. If we compare his pretreatment and posttreatment behavior, there were dramatic changes. You might object that the change could have been due to other sources, such as Dicky getting older. As we pointed out in the case study of the young woman with a bridge phobia, one case study alone does not prove anything. The case must be understood in the larger context of related studies. Dicky was being compared indirectly with a large number of control subjects. Many other children with specific behavior problems did not get treated and did not improve. In another sense, Dicky was being

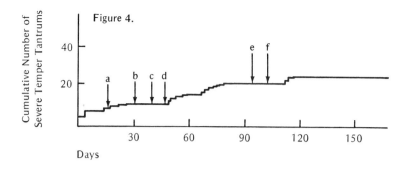

Figure 4.

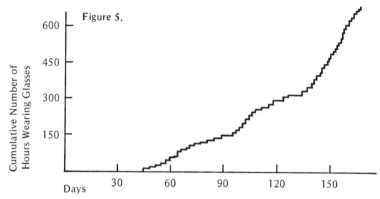

Figure 5.

Figures 4 and 5 represent cumulative response curves. A portion of the curve which is horizontal indicates that *no responses* were made during the time covered by that portion. Thus, in Figure 4, no severe temper tantrums at all were made after about the 115th day. The slope of the cumulative curve is a direct measure of the rate of responding. The shape of the curve in Figure 5 indicates that, generally speaking, once Dicky got started wearing glasses, he wore them for longer periods each day, until he leveled off at about the 150th day at a rate of 12 hours per day.

compared indirectly with many other kinds of control subjects. The investigators were using a set of very highly controlled conditions that were developed in hundreds of laboratories on thousands of subjects of many species. These conditions—the rewards, punishments, and stimuli that accompany them—have been studied on a multitude of controls, from mice to pigeons to children to adults.

Before bringing this study back to our original question, let us consider a possible error in interpretation. The fact that Dicky's disturbed behavior can be modified through the use of learning principles does *not* necessarily mean that this disturbed behavior was learned. Some biologically determined behaviors can be changed by learning. Just consider the effects described in the section on voodoo death. The kind of disorder Dicky had may have been biological, or it may have been learned. No one knows.

This study and the tradition it represents speaks to the first half of our grand question, Why does one's personality change under stress? It points to the importance of the situation, as a source of control over behavior. But it speaks more directly to the question, How can psychologists help? The answer it suggests goes well beyond specific operations for a particular kind of case. The answer involves a clear scientific position about how we can think about maladaptive behavior. It suggests that the *behavior* itself should be the target of our therapies—that we should *change the behavior*. This is an important issue, one to which we will return in Part III.

BRIEF DESCRIPTIONS OF OTHER STUDIES

In the preceding sections we have presented fourteen research studies in some depth. Those that were related to why personality changes under stress employed a variety of definitions of stress, ranging from electric shock to immersion in water. The definitions of change in personality varied from answers to a questionnaire to ulceration and death. The investigators used many different kinds of subjects, including rats, monkeys, and people. Those studies primarily concerned with how psychologists can help used a wide variety of techniques aimed at changing behavior. We have selected a variety of approaches since we wanted to demonstrate the breadth and complexity of one student's original question. Even though variety was one of the criteria by which we selected studies, we have really presented only a minute sampling of the literature, only a handful of the experiments and case studies that have been published. Thousands of research studies dealing with the effects of stress are published every year. Thousands more deal with how psychologists can help.

We want to demonstrate further the complexity of the original grand question. We will briefly present a few other investigations into the effects of stress and into methods of helping. Again, you should be aware that we are just scratching the surface.

The U.S. Navy has been conducting a major research program centering on the ability of people to live and work for long periods of time under the sea. A significant aspect of this program involves the attempt to assess the psychological impact of the multiple, unusual stresses involved in undersea life. The psychological components of this project are discussed in a fascinating book, *Groups Under Stress: Psychological Research in Sealab II* (Radloff & Helmreich, 1968). The book details men's reactions, not only to the environmental stresses involved in living undersea and going on long diving missions outside their habitat, but also to the social stresses of living together in close quarters over extended periods of time.

Ruff and Korchin (1964) discuss research on the environmental stresses involved in exploring *space*. They investigated not only the life history and personality characteristics of the Mercury astronauts but also their responses to the stresses of space flight.

R. S. Lazarus (1964) presents some laboratory research in which the stress was showing the subjects a film of a very crude, very painful ritual operation on the genitals of adolescent boys in a primitive society. In this research the reactions observed were psychophysiological responses, such as those described in Johnson's research above.

The psychiatrist R. J. Lifton (1964) presents his analysis of the long-term psychological effects of the atomic bomb blast on those who survived Hiroshima. Lifton went to Japan seventeen years after the nuclear explosion and interviewed a large number of people who had been there. Even after seventeen years, the influences of the disaster were so profound that Lifton reported that the *interviews* left *him* shocked and emotionally spent.

The effects of a most extreme form of stress—internment in a concentration camp—is discussed by Biderman (1964). C. B. Bahnsen (1964) also explores reactions to the threat of annihilation, recalling some of his own emotional responses as he fled and hid from the Nazi Gestapo in World War II. He analyzes the written reflections of a young Danish freedom fighter who made notes between torture sessions before he was killed by the Gestapo.

In one way or another every investigation we have presented thus far has involved the observation of some behavioral change in the organism that seemed to be a consequence of some environmental event—of some change or difference in the environment. In many of the studies, the environment was deliberately manipulated by the investigator. In others, especially some of those just cited, the investigator made observations after some environmental event *not* under experimental control had occurred.

A series of studies by S. B. Sarason and his colleagues takes a still different tack (Sarason, Davidson, Lighthall, Waite, & Ruebush, 1960). This research into the question of why a person's personality changes under stress is not aimed at predicting behavior from differences in the environment, but rather it is aimed at predicting how different individuals will behave differently, given a stressful environmental event. Sarason has focused upon performance on examinations and how that performance is affected by the anxiety of the test-takers. He approached the problem by using paper-and-pencil psychological tests to measure what he called "test-anxiety." He and his colleagues developed a questionnaire specifically designed to tap this construct; they called it the Test-Anxiety Questionnaire. They demonstrated that the children who responded differently to their questionnaire did perform differently on examinations and did react differently to anxiety-manipulating instructions. The students' performance on school tests differed as predicted by their questionnaire performance even though the students were equivalent in what are generally considered to be the determiners of academic achievement.

A thorough description of this research would require an entire section like those presented previously in Part II, but the essential character of Sarason's work should be clear from what has been said. Sarason was not looking at behavioral differences that result from an environmental event, like shock. Rather, he was looking at differences in the behavior of different subjects in relation to the same environmental event, an examination.

Brief descriptions of investigations on stress and personality could continue almost indefinitely. We have not even mentioned some entire areas of stress research, such as stresses in business organizations (e.g., Kahn, Wolfe, Quinn, & Snoek, 1964; McGrath, 1976), investigations of specific coping responses to stress (Coelho, Hamburg, & Adams, 1974), studies of urban (Glass & Singer, 1972) and prison (Toch, 1975) stresses, attempts to relate stress to other constructs (e.g., Broadbent, 1971), and military stress research (e.g., Grinker & Spiegel, 1945; Basowitz, Persky, Korchin, & Grinker, 1955). Numerous conferences have been devoted to the topic of stress. For example, Appley and Trumbull (1967) brought together scientists to discuss physiological, psychophysiological, emotional, cognitive, and social aspects of stress.

What about the question, How can psychologists help? In choosing studies relevant to this question we decided that the clinical material we would present in Part II would be a highly selective sample, representing only the behavioral approach. This selection procedure was used not because we believe this strategy is the only or best approach to helping, but rather because investigators in the behavioral tradition present materials in a way that made it possible for us to summarize the work more easily. Let's now look at a short but somewhat wider sampling of the various strategies clinical psychologists use in trying to help.

The kind of treatment people receive when they go to a clinical psychologist for help varies not only with the kind of problem they are experiencing but also with the psychologist's own orientation toward helping. Keeping this in mind, we can try to give you some idea of the major kinds of helping techniques currently being applied and investigated.

Children who are experiencing the effects of stress are helped in a variety of ways. Recall our example of Dicky in the preceding section where psychologists applied reinforcement principles directly to the child in an effort to teach him some specific responses. In recent years considerable work has been aimed at helping children by having psychologists teach parents and teachers how to apply the same behavior modification principles in the home or classroom (Patterson,

1969). This is, of course, an extension of the basic behavioral approach.

A different method of helping children is play therapy. Here the psychologist works individually with the child (e.g., Harrison, 1975) or with a small group of children (e.g., Ginott, 1961). The general goals of the play therapy approach are to use play to help children work through and understand their feelings about themselves and their environment, thereby developing new and more efficient ways of getting along.

Very often entire families are experiencing stress and are worked with as a unit (Haley, 1975). Here the psychologist meets regularly with a couple and their children. They all discuss problems occurring within the family. The goals are to reduce family stress. A similar approach to treating stresses in a marriage is for the husband and wife to meet with a therapist in marriage counseling sessions (Sadock, 1975). The sessions are aimed at helping a man and woman resolve problems that exist between the two of them, problems that often threaten the marriage itself.

All the above approaches are used often. However, when people think of how psychologists help they most often think of individual psychotherapy, in which a person meets the therapist regularly and talks about personal difficulties. Individual therapy itself takes a variety of forms depending upon the patient's problems and the psychologist's orientation (Wolberg, 1967). In general, the overall goals are (1) to help the patient understand and resolve his or her problems and (2) to develop new and more efficient ways of reacting to himself or herself and to the environment. These same goals are sought in group psychotherapy for adults (e.g., Yalom, 1970). Here the therapist meets simultaneously with a small group of patients. He or she uses the group members' reactions to each other and to the group to change behavior.

These approaches (and many more) are currently being studied by researchers in an effort to determine their effectiveness with different problems and to determine how they might be changed to increase that effectiveness.

Part III Beyond Specific Answers

I n Part I of this book you read a list of broad questions asked by students on the first day of an introductory psychology class. We selected a two-part question and analyzed it word for word. In the remainder of that section we tried to show you that such questions are scientifically unanswerable. In Part II we presented a number of questions related to the one analyzed in Part I. These questions were answerable because the investigators had reduced them to specific operations. We contrasted the differences between the answerable questions attacked by these investigators and the unanswerable ones often asked by people who are not researchers. Furthermore, we tried to provide examples that would represent the diversity of the methods of attack and, at the same time, some of the essential similarities underlying all of the diverse methods.

In Part III we will use the research studies of Part II as examples to make explicit some important ideas about the science of behavior. While we will use many of the studies as illustrations of each point, we will *not* attempt to exhaust all possible examples from Part II.

THREE CHARACTERISTICS OF BEHAVIORAL RESEARCH

I n this section we will discuss three characteristics of research. The first of these, objective observation, is an absolutely essential feature of all scientific research. The second, control (depending upon how broadly the term is defined), may be considered either as an essential characteristic of scientific research or as a characteristic of an important form of research—*experimental* research. While control is one of those words that means different things in different contexts, the meaning in each one of the contexts is precise and clear. While the third feature of research we will discuss, quantification, is *not* a necessary feature of science, it is a commonly used and powerful tool in research.

Objective Observation

Recall the very first comment we made in Part I after we noted that the student's question, as posed, could not be answered scientifically. That comment was, "Before a question can be considered scientifically meaningful, it must be asked in such a fashion that a scientist can make the *observations* necessary to answer it." The term *observation* was then tied to objectivity, which was defined as the extent to which different observers agree on what happened. The research studies in Part II illustrate over and over again the definition and measurement of concepts in terms of objective observations made under controlled conditions.

The very first study in Part II deals with one of Freud's hypotheses. It exemplifies an extreme reduction of theoretical concepts to observations upon which people could agree. Hunt's manipulation of "feeding frustration" could be checked by an independent observer. His definition of feeding frustration was in terms of the length of time the subjects went without food and the brief periods of time (10 minutes) they were allowed to eat. His definition of adulthood was also one that other investigators could agree on—not in the sense that they would necessarily agree that six months constituted adulthood, but in the sense that they could agree when a rat born on a particular day was six months old. The same is true for Hunt's sharply "reduced" definition of "orality" in adult personality, which was hoarding. Different observers could certainly agree on the number of pellets an experimental or control rat hoarded, even though they may disagree sharply as to whether or not hoarding was a measure of "orality."

Objectivity not only makes it possible for other investigators to repeat the observations (repeatability) but also determines the actual meaning of the terms as defined by the experimental operations of the investigator. That is, objectivity provides operational definitions of key terms.

Similarly, Brady's manipulation of stress could be checked by independent observers. The investigator carefully designed the experimental situation in such a way that allowed different people to agree that the monkeys were in restraint chairs, getting shocked, pressing levers, and so on. Brady's study also illustrates that certain forms of observation require special competence. It takes training to recognize ulcers in a monkey's stomach.

The application of the concept of objectivity is easily apparent in most of the reports. Schachter defined anxiety by instructions and affiliation by a rating scale. An independent observer could have noted that he did in fact give such instructions and that a 5 on the rating scale was indeed a 5. Schachter did *not* report that he had watched the subjects and *thought* that they would have liked some company. He used a rating scale to evaluate their affiliative needs *objectively*. The investigation of conflict reduction by Balke, Hammond, and Meyer illustrates objectivity in an especially clear way. We usually think of the reasons underlying people's judgments as being private and subjective. But these reasons may be investigated by the judgment analysis performed in the Balke et al. research. That is, the weighting scheme used may be made "open to inspection." What was a private, subjective weighting scheme is made public and objectively observable. As a result, different observers could agree on the issues a person considered important in making judgments and on just how important that person considered those issues.

Cannon's and Shurley's research pose some difficulties for this discussion of objectivity. Since the problem raised by Shurley's sensory isolation study is both more difficult and more interesting, we'll deal with Cannon's study first! Recall that Cannon did not go out and "run subjects" as did the other investigators. He carefully reviewed the literature on voodoo death and brought his expert knowledge of physiology to bear on that literature. He did not himself make the observations, but he was aware of the need for establishing the objectivity of the data he used. He referred to available records of medical examinations and to postmortem reports. He looked for similar reports of the relevant behaviors by individuals in cultures that were not in any form of contact with one another. Finally, he related these observations by others—the objectivity of which he could not directly assess—to the highly objective observations routinely made in the physiological laboratory.

The problem raised by Shurley's research is a fundamental one when dealing with the requirement of objective observation. One of the measures of behavior that Shurley used was the number of hours each subject spent in the water-filled chamber. That, of course, provides no problem in terms of objectivity. Different people doing the timing would obtain almost identical results. But recall that Shurley also talked about dreams and about hallucinations. How does an independent observer check on the objectivity of a report that a subject saw herself as an iced-tea spoon, slowly stirring a glass of iced tea? How does one evaluate whether the physician "really" heard the snapping of his aortic valve?

It is simply not possible to establish objectively the content of an hallucination, or even the fact that a subject experiences one. Nor is it possible to establish objectively the content of a dream. The actual objective results of Shurley's investigations into the effects of sensory deprivation are, from a scientific point of view, not that his subjects had hallucinations but that they *stated verbally* that they had hallucinations. On those reports, independent scientific investigators can agree; that is, they can agree that a subject said she saw herself as an iced-tea spoon, slowly stirring a glass of iced tea. From the perspective of scientific objectivity, the observer will never know just what *private experience* the subject was having at the time of the report. Of course, the scientist almost certainly believes that the hallucinations are real and bases much work on that assumption.

This distinction may seem to be a quibble, a playing with words. It is not. It is an important distinction that has special relevance to all psychological research which makes inferences from what people say. This issue may be especially acute in the area of clinical research, where we must be aware that patients may claim that they are "better" for a wide variety of reasons, only one of which may be that they are functioning more effectively. You have read how the sections dealing with clinical problems achieved objectivity. Wolf, Risley, and Mees defined Dicky's "tantrums" in terms of specific behaviors (head-banging, face-scratching, hair-pulling). Glasses-wearing is directly observable, and it was timed. Silverman and Geer not only asked the patient if she still feared crossing bridges but also watched her cross one. Budzynski and his colleagues had subjects rate their headaches on a 5-point scale. The objective data of the investigation were the ratings rather than the subjective intensity of headaches. Davidson's objective observations in his study of snake phobia were how close, in terms of his 13-step hierarchy, each phobic person would come to the snake.

You can easily go back to the few studies we have not used as examples and see how the investigators took abstract terms and reduced their definitions to observables. They reduced them to events that other people could have agreed, "Yes, that did happen." The same can be done for any scientific investigation you study in your reading in psychology. Without such objective observation of the relevant events, however cleverly the investigation may be done, it is not science. In situations in which there is any doubt about the occurrence of some event or of its magnitude, *multiple, independent* observers are routinely used, and measures of reliability (objectivity) routinely reported.

Without objective observation, it's not good science, it's not even bad science—it's not science at all.

Control

One of the major characteristics of any scientific investigation is *control*. In its broadest sense, control refers in part to the conditions of observation briefly discussed in the section above. Astronomy is a highly developed science relying on exquisitely controlled conditions of observation. But there is another usage of the term *control*, generally expressed as *experimental control*. In that usage, control refers to those operations performed when an experimenter is manipulating an aspect of the environment, which for the moment we shall call A, and keeping constant (controlling) other possible influences (B, C, D, and others) on the behavior of interest. Thus in the present context, control does not refer to the ability to direct, or guide, or control behavior in the way that Wolf, Risley, and Mees achieved control over Dicky's temper tantrums. Rather, control refers to experimental operations that enable us to say, after we have carried out an experiment, that it was factor A which led to the results, not factors B, C, D, or E. All scientific experiments include control operations. This is true even though the nature of these operations may vary greatly from experiment to experiment.

One basic technique by which control may be achieved is through the use of control groups. Control groups permit the researcher to make comparisons between the effects of the particular manipulation being investigated and the effects of other manipulations, or between manipulation and no manipulation at all. All factors are kept constant across groups of subjects—everything except the specific manipulation that is under examination. Another basic technique for providing such comparisons is by use of the subject as his or her own control. While the operations involved for the subject-as-own-control design are different from the control-group design, both are conceptually very similar and each presents some special problems. Researchers may choose to obtain the needed control comparisons by using either of the two approaches. With this brief, general background in mind, let's now examine how the principle of control is exemplified in the research presented in Part II.

The control-group technique is illustrated by Hunt's investigation of the effects of infant feeding frustration on adult hoarding behavior. In order to evaluate his hypothesis, Hunt made comparisons between different groups of rats. Recall that he compared the hoarding behavior of rats that were frustrated in infancy with rats that did not receive this treatment in early life. In order to evaluate the "early age" part of the hypothesis, Hunt needed other control groups that provided comparisons between early and later feeding frustration with respect to hoarding behavior. If he had not used these control groups, he could not have drawn the inferences from the research that he did. Except for the particular manipulation of interest, the control groups were treated exactly the same as the experimental groups.

Control groups were used in a very similar manner by Masserman in his efforts to determine the role of conflict in the development of experimental neuroses, by Johnson in his study of physiological arousal, by Schachter in his work on affiliation, and by Davidson in his study of systematic desensitization.

While many researchers use groups of subjects to attain control, the specific way in which these groups are used varies greatly. The variations are dependent upon both the nature of the question being asked and the factor to be controlled. We can look at Brady's work on ulceration. His control group was made up of a number of monkeys that were yoked individually to experimental, or "executive," monkeys. Brady thus had the comparison he needed to evaluate his data. He could make postmortem comparisons between the stomachs of animals that had been required to respond in order to avoid shock and those that had not been required to make such a response. Each yoked control animal had the same experiences as the experimental partner except that the control animal could not make the response that avoided shock. When compared to their experimental partners, the yoked controls experienced equal shock, equal time in a restraining chair, equal lighting in the experimental room, and so forth. The only difference was that the control subjects could not respond in order to avoid shock. The executive monkeys could. Another possible source of variation also held constant is probably obvious. The animals were all rhesus monkeys. Therefore, possible species differences were eliminated. Along the same lines, the use of animals ensured that there were no significant differences in the subjects' past history which could have accounted for ulceration when it occurred. One reason for using animals as subjects is that we usually know or have controlled their past history. Many research questions require that we have very specific knowledge of our subject's developmental and psychological past.

In addition to experiments in which specific groups are used to achieve control, many researchers employ the "subjects-as-their-own-control" design. When control groups are used, the essential question is, How does the behavior of the experimental group differ from the behavior of the control group? For example, do rats frustrated in infancy hoard more than nonfrustrated ones? Often it is more convenient, more efficient, or more appropriate to use subjects as their own controls. When a research question is approached with this type of design, the question might be phrased, Does a subject's (or group of subjects') behavior *change* as a function of a specific experimental manipulation? In this type of experimental design, the researcher observes some selected aspect of the subjects' behavior at a specific time, then carries out his or her experimental manipulation on these same subjects, and then again observes their behavior. No separate control groups are used, for the subjects are literally their own control groups. Many questions can be approached with either of the above designs.

Miller's research provides an example of the subjects-as-their-own-control design. In order to test his hypothesis, Miller chose to carry his experiment out in a series of steps or stages. His first step was to demonstrate that the white compartment was a neutral stimulus. The final step demonstrated that rats would learn a novel response, wheel-turning, to escape this previously neutral compartment. The important point for our present purpose is that all of the steps were carried out with the *same* rats. Step one provided control comparisons for step two, and so forth. This will be very clear if you will refer back to the section entitled, "Can Learning Create Stress Situations?" and look at the comparisons made as Miller's research progressed from step-to-step.

Wolf, Risley, and Mees' work with Dicky provides an important example of a subject used as his own control. Before the treatment procedures were carried out, the boy had temper tantrums and refused to wear his glasses. It was possible to demonstrate systematic changes in Dicky's behavior as the work progressed and to argue that these changes were due to the manipulations performed on Dicky.

You should be aware that this is really a partial control operation. That is, it could be argued that Dicky's behavior might have changed anyway, perhaps as a function of his simply getting older. For reasons like this, researchers often use what is called a *reversal design* when subjects are used as their own control. Most simply put, this design entails: (1) observing the behavior of interest *prior* to any experimental manipulation, (2) instituting the manipulation and observing any changes in that behavior, (3) ceasing the manipulation while continuing to observe the behavior, and then (4) reinstituting the manipulation. The researcher can then make comparisons between the times when the manipulations were in effect and the times when no such operations were being applied. This makes it possible to determine if it was some aspect of the experimental operations that produced behavior changes. In cases like Dicky's or in other clinical studies like Silverman and Geer's treatment of the girl with a bridge phobia, researchers are highly reluctant to use such reversal designs. You can see why. If the operations seem to be working to reduce the distress that led the patient to seek help, it is not in the patient's best interests to stop the treatment in order to see if the problem returns. This means, of course, that in many real-life clinical case studies we have imperfect experimental control. However, this is a trade-off that must often be made.

What about Cannon's study of "voodoo" death? Remember that the purpose of using controls is to rule out alternative explanations of the findings. Cannon did attempt this. Through a careful review of the literature he tried to rule out deaths due to old age, poison, disease, and so forth. He used the *concept* of control by searching out data that would allow him to rule out other possible interpretations of the phenomenon. Again, as in the clinical case study research, this is far from perfect control. It is clearly not experimental control, and we must be cautious in our interpretations of data gathered under these circumstances. But it is important to note that the nature of Cannon's question was such that really sound experimental controls were not possible. Again, a trade-off. We will be returning to this trade-off issue later.

There are many control techniques that we have not presented. In order to ensure comparability of groups so that differences can be attributed to the experimental manipulation, researchers randomly assign subjects to groups or make up matched groups. The latter is accomplished by carefully selecting and assigning subjects to groups on the basis of some characteristic relevant to the study. In some experiments it is necessary to control for effects like practice over time. A technique known as counterbalancing is used in those situations.

It is not our purpose to outline or explain all the possible approaches that one may take to obtain control. Rather it is our purpose to emphasize the importance of control in scientific research. While control has many forms, the fundamental purpose is the same.

Without adequate controls we cannot meaningfully interpret research data.

Quantification

The section above on the use of objective observation to define, identify, and measure concepts in psychological research provides a perfect background for our discussion of quantification. Most simply, quantification means assigning numbers to observations. These numbers may be test scores; they may be counts telling us how many times a certain event occurred. They may be dosage levels of a drug or the number of shocks an animal gets at a certain level of intensity. In this sense quantification is intimately bound to observation and to making observations in an objective way, a way that ensures agreement among observers.

Quantification is also intimately tied to another concept that we introduced early in Part I when we discussed the word *change*. Behavior change is most easily described in scientific terms if the particular actions we are observing are quantified. In the laboratory study of students with snake phobias, Davidson described the reduction of subjects' fear of snakes in terms of the *number* of steps in his behavioral test the subjects would complete after treatment as compared to the number prior to treatment.

Quantification enters the scientific picture right at the very outset. Big questions must be reduced to answerable ones by defining the terms of the question by observables. *Most* scientists have a very strong preference for using quantitative definitions whenever possible. If you will mull over the studies presented, you will see that this aspect of quantification has been implicitly presented time and time again throughout this book.

Consider the following illustrations of this point drawn from the studies reviewed. Hunt defined *young* in quantitative terms, number of days since weaning, and he defined *hoarding* quantitatively as well, in terms of the number of pellets.

Brady reported shock level in quantitative terms and *counted* the number of experimental monkeys that developed ulcers as opposed to the number of yoked controls that developed ulcers. At this point it may be well to note that Brady had alternatives available other than counting. He could have measured the extent of the ulceration and calculated average amount of ulceration or he could have used some other more elaborate measurement technique. He chose simply to count ulcerated monkeys.

Schachter, in the portions of his research that we reported, did not attempt to quantify his manipulation of the environment. He gave the female students two different sets of instructions and reported a verbatim transcription of these instructions in his book. He did, however, present a quantitative statement of his measure of behavior. While he simply asked the subjects if they would rather wait alone or wait with someone else, he evaluated his hypothesis by the difference in *num-*

bers between those who said they would rather be alone in the various conditions and those who said they would rather be with someone else.

Johnson carefully specified his conflict manipulations in quantitative terms, detailing the number of metronome beats per second. He also defined *arousal* in a quantitative fashion, measuring and reporting heart rate, skin conductance, and palmar sweat. Miller, too, and Wolf, Risley, and Mees employed quantification as an integral, crucial part of their research designs.

Reporting observations quantitatively rather than qualitatively permits great precision and repeatability. Silverman and Geer were concerned with the *number* of nightmares their patient had before, during, and after treatment. Budzynski and his associates studied the effects of biofeedback as a prescription for headaches, and they expressed that effectiveness in terms of how the *rated* intensity of headaches was reduced. That is, they asked the patients to quantify the subjective experience of pain by assigning a number to each headache they experienced. The higher the number the worse the headache.

You will recall that in the study of TV watching and violence, the relationship between these two events was expressed in terms of correlation coefficients—numerical values that described the *strength* of a relationship. In this study aggressive behavior was rated (that is, assigned a number) as was the level of violence of the TV programs that mothers reported their children preferred.

The conflict reduction study provides another example of the use of quantification in research. The negotiator quantified the issues on the contracts in terms of how important he thought each was to him. The negotiators' quantified judgments of the individual contracts were processed in a computer so that he and others could objectively observe the actual judgment policy he was utilizing.

Not all investigators, nor even all of those we have mentioned, are interested in problems that are easily reducible to quantifiable terms. Shurley, for example, expressed neither his manipulation nor his measure of behavior in quantitative terms. He did present a careful verbal description of the tank and associated apparatus and gave some verbatim accounts of what the subjects said while in the tank.

You may have noted that we have been classifying under the labels *quantification* and *measurement* some rather different methods for assigning numbers to observations. In some of the cases events either occurred or did not occur and were counted. As far as Brady was concerned, monkeys either ulcerated or they did not. Conversely, Hunt was concerned with *how many* pellets each rat hoarded, not *whether or not* the rat hoarded. They all hoarded to some extent, but knowing how much each one hoarded enabled Hunt to assess the effects of infant feeding frustration. All of Johnson's subjects had measurable skin conductances, but the values of the measures differed drastically from person to person and from group to group. Therefore, he had to measure the degree, not the presence or absence, of skin conductance. There are, in fact, several different categories of measurement. Just how much one can do with the numbers depends in part on the type of measurement used, but to discuss these here would be too much of a digression. The point is that *many* investigators strive to define their manipulations and their measures of behavior so that numerical values can be used to represent them.

Quantification plays another major role in science, one which we have not illustrated in the studies cited. This role is at the theoretical level and involves mathematical descriptions of the relationships among the major constructs of a science. The really powerful examples of this role of quantification as a theoretical tool must be borrowed from other sciences. Perhaps the most impressive, well-known examples are from the fields of astronomy and physics. Think for a while about the astonishing theoretical feats accomplished with the aid of mathematics in the field of astronomy. Multitudes of observations over the centuries have been made on the motions of the planets, the moon, and the stars. We now know that the distances and speeds involved are so great that the term *astronomical* has come into general use as representing numbers that are almost inconceivably large. And yet the astronomers, in developing a theory of how the universe functions, have written complex equations describing the orbits of celestial bodies so accurately that rockets can be sent off from the earth which will land on the moon or on a planet. This requires aiming the rocket at a location in space to which the target will not even be close for months. Multitudes of observations by astronomers have been neatly organized by the mathematical equations. As you may know, the astronomer's equations not only nicely organized existing knowledge about astronomic phenomena but also enabled astronomers to predict the existence of the previously unobserved planets, Neptune and Pluto.

Psychologists, too, are attempting to express their theories in a quantitative fashion, but nothing they have yet produced matches these elegant descriptions of astronomical phenomena. What mathematical theories or models there are in psychology are intended to describe only very limited aspects of behavior. For example, there are relatively precise and well-established mathematical expressions in the areas of sensation, decision-making, and simple learning. Quantification enters the research picture in another way: the use of statistical methods to evaluate data. We will be returning to this in a later section.

The quantitative expression of scientific questions, theories, and hypotheses has many advantages that recall the advantages of quantitative defintions. If a theory is expressed quantitatively, it can be tested precisely. Conversely, theories that are stated only in verbal terms can all too often be interpreted very differently by different people. To the extent that this is the case, such theories cannot be tested precisely.

So quantification enters into science at every stage of the game. It plays an essential role in the definition of the terms used in asking questions about nature, in the gathering and analysis of the evidence, and in our theorizing as well.

RESEARCH STRATEGIES

s you saw in Part II of this book, there are many different ways of investigating answerable questions. The research methodologies ranged from creating whole, artificial environments in which stimulation was reduced to a minimum, to reading accounts of strange deaths that had been reported by other investigators.

The apparatus utilized by the investigators included boxes with grid floors and black and white walls (Miller), phony shock apparatus (Schachter), special restraining chairs (Brady), test booklets (Sarason), a nonpoisonous snake (Davidson), and a half-gallon of ice cream (Wolf, Risley, & Mees)! Other investigators utilized no apparatus as such; they explored the effects of stress on personality by going into real-life situations where great stresses were known to have occurred, as in the study on the long-term effects of the atomic bombing of Hiroshima.

Similarly, the subjects used in the studies presented in Part II varied considerably. The subject populations from which the samples were selected included rats, monkeys, and people.

Can we categorize research in a more basic and important way than in terms of differences among the subjects used, the apparatus employed, and the content area involved? The answer is Yes! In this section, we will focus on one of the major distinctions, that between *manipulative* and *nonmanipulative* research. This is a significant distinction in psychology. The distinction often goes under the name of experimental (manipulative) versus nonexperimental research. Most of the sections in Part II were devoted to descriptions of research in which the experimenter manipulated the subjects' environment in some way. Hunt deprived his rats of food. Brady manipulated the degree to which his monkeys could influence what was happening to them as they received electric shock. Schachter threatened his subjects with shock. Miller shocked his rats in a specially constructed environment. Shurley created an entirely artificial environment for his subjects, immersing them in a tank of water. Masserman deprived his cats of food and stimulated them with electric shocks and air blasts. Johnson required a difficult discrimination as he stimulated his students with electric shocks. Wolf, Risley, and Mees manipulated Dicky's environment by making the delivery of food contingent upon certain specific behaviors. They also went to the trouble of instructing everybody around Dicky just how to respond to him when he behaved in certain ways. Balke, Hammond, and Meyer tried to influence the behavior of their negotiators by providing them with feedback. The therapists in the two sections on fear reduction instructed fear-ridden individuals on the use of a fear hierarchy and relaxation, and Budzynski and his co-workers manipulated their subjects with biofeedback apparatus.

These investigators selected a particular factor in the subjects' environment and manipulated it systematically. They then observed those aspects of the subjects' behavior in which they were interested. One special form of manipulative investigation is called *experimental* research. In experiments, not only is the factor of interest manipulated, but other potential influences are held strictly constant by the experimenter. We would like to emphasize the importance of the experiment by summarizing it in its ideal form:

1. Vary or manipulate an aspect of the environment.
2. Hold other aspects of the environment constant.
3. Observe any changes in the subjects' behavior.
4. See if the changes in the subjects' behavior are associated with changes in the subjects' environment.

The typical clinical case study, such as Silverman and Geer's treatment of bridge phobia, is manipulative but is *not* a formal experiment. We chose to emphasize manipulative research in Part II for several reasons. The nature of the first part of the grand question, How does personality change under stress? is such that it lends itself nicely to manipulative research. So does the second, How can psychologists help? The selection of a few studies from thousands of possibilities reflects the authors' biases. It is our belief, and the belief of many other psychologists, that whenever a research question can be appropriately attacked experimentally, the experimental approach is preferable to other approaches. The reason can be expressed in one word, *control*. The experimental method provides the greatest degree of control. In the experimental method the particular condition of interest is manipulated. At the same time other conditions that may potentially affect the consequent behavior of interest—but with which the investigator is not concerned at the moment—can be controlled right out of the experiment. Because of this characteristic, the experimentally oriented investigator can often isolate precisely which antecedent condition is influencing the subjects' behavior. Thus experimental research can yield cause-effect relations. Hunt could say with considerable certainty that it was the deprivation of food at an early age that *caused* hoarding in the adult rats; Brady could say that requiring the monkeys to avoid shock was a *causal* agent in ulcer development, and so on.

Some of the manipulative studies we presented were not adequately controlled because the nature of the question addressed placed limitations on the experimenter's ability to exercise control. The study on conflict reduction by Balke, Hammond, and Meyer was manipulative, but the lack of an adequate number of subjects prevents an investigator from making strong causal statements based on that study alone. Silverman and Geer performed manipulations to reduce the young woman's bridge phobia, but they did not have sufficient control *within* that one investigation to establish scientifically a causal relation between the therapy and the improvement. We do not wish to sound too negative by dwelling on examples of imperfect control. A well-designed experiment allows an unambiguous statement of a cause-effect relationship. Nevertheless, certain research is important to do even when adequate control is not possible.

Experimental research is a powerful tool in the hands of an imaginative scientist. But it is not the only tool. Scientists use a variety of other methods, several of which were presented in Part II. One of the major forms of nonmanipulative research is called *correlational research*. It involves careful observation and measurement of two or more different aspects of the subjects' behavior and then a determination of whether or not these different aspects are related in any systematic way.

If correlational research does lead to statements of lawful relationships between two aspects of behavior, it enables the investigator to make predictions about behavior. That is, the investigator can predict, with some accuracy, one aspect of behavior from knowledge of another aspect of behavior. For example, if there is a known, lawful relationship between grades in mathematics courses and grades in physics courses, then one could predict physics grades by knowing math grades. The predictions would not be perfect, but they would be better, on the average, than predictions made without using the math grades. This kind of knowledge—knowledge about the relationship between behaviors—can be extraordinarily valuable in situations where one of the behaviors is easy to observe and measure, and the other is extremely difficult, or very costly, to obtain. An actual example of correlational research in just such a situation involves the development by the U.S. Air Force of a paper-and-pencil test to predict success in pilot-training school. A paper-and-pencil test is very cheap and it is easy to give. With the large group on which the Air Force developed the test, it was found by correlational research that the test predicted remarkably well which members of the group would ultimately "wash out" of pilot-training school. In this case prediction means that a person who attains a high score on the test is very likely to succeed in training, while an individual who gets a low score is likely to fail. In this original group on which the correlational research was done, everyone was tested and went on to pilot-training school. But the practical use of the test came with later groups. Since the test predicted success and failure well in the original group, it was assumed that the test would predict success and failure of subsequent applicants as well. This assumption could be made since the characteristics of the applicants did not change in any systematic fashion and since the training program stayed the same. The test results could therefore be used as one important source of information in deciding whether to accept or reject an applicant. Thus in the thousands of cases after the test was developed, the inexpensive, easy-to-get test score was used in the selection of applicants, and a much smaller proportion washed out. Not only is the training school spared the large expense of partially training someone only to see that person fail to complete the program, but also many individuals are spared the major disappointment involved in failing. Errors are certainly made. Some applicants who are selected do not make it. Some who are rejected would have made it had they been accepted. But the errors in selection are fewer than would have been the case had the test not been developed and used.

Notice that there is no attempt to make statements of a causal nature. Such statements would be irrelevant, as you will see if you try to phrase one. Does performance on the test "cause" success or failure in flight training school? That question makes no sense. The research that led to this particular test was not concerned with answering a causal question.

Examples of correlational research abound in the psychological literature. Prediction of college grades from college-board scores is somewhat successful because much research was done in which the predictor tests and the predicted behaviors were correlated. Prediction of school success from IQ tests also rests upon many years of such correlational research. In all of these instances, a very hard-to-get segment of behavior is predicted from a much more accessible segment, test scores.

It should be clear why the typical correlational study cannot lead to certain knowledge about cause and effect, even in studies in which causal questions are raised. Consider Lifton's research, reported in the final section of Part II. When Lifton interviewed the atomic bomb survivors, he found lingering effects after a seventeen-year span. We can ask, Effects of what? Lifton himself pointed out that the survivors were given a special name by their neighbors and were regarded as inferior in some ways. Changes in their behavior had taken place. But were the behavioral changes due to the massive shock experienced at the moment of impact or to seeing the unparalleled suffering in the aftermath of the bomb? Or perhaps even to radiation-induced biological differences? Or, as implied above, perhaps the effects were due to the long-term discrimination against the victims by those not directly affected by the bomb. There is no way of knowing.

Nonmanipulative methods are, however, often used in an attempt to gather data relevant to causal questions, simply because the nature of the question precludes the use of controlled experiments. The two most clear cases of nonmanipulative research presented in Part II are Cannon's study of voodoo death and the study relating TV violence and aggression. A careful reading of these two sections will reveal that in neither case was the investigator able to manipulate and control the environment. In neither case was a strong statement made about cause-effect relations, but rather the conclusion in each was that the results were *consistent with* a particular causal interpretation. In fact, one reason the TV violence study was selected for presentation in Part II of this book is precisely because it was an attempt to do a non-manipulative, correlational study on a question dealing with a causal relationship. Sophisticated statistical analyses were performed to rule out some possible interpretations, but still the nonexperimental nature of the study does not permit anyone to make the flat statement that the later aggression was *caused* by the exposure to violence on TV.

This statement about the inability of nonmanipulative research to yield cause-effect relationships is not meant to devalue correlational methodology. If you will reflect upon the examples of nonmanipulative research, you will see that many interesting, important, and answerable questions are simply not amenable to experimental manipulation. In fact, entire fields of science—astronomy for one—do not employ any sort of manipulative methodology. In psychology one of the many classes of questions that must be approached correlationally involves the development of psychological tests as exemplified above. How could an investigator employ manipulative research in attacking the problem of predicting who will be successful in pilot training? What is needed for the prediction is some measure of the performance of the applicant from which pilot training performance can be predicted. This is essentially the definition of correlational research—the prediction of one kind of performance from another, the prediction of one kind of behavior from another. If you will consider the other research questions advanced previously in the illustrations of non-manipulative research, you will see that they simply cannot be approached by the experimental method. How can we experimentally study voodoo death or the influence of atomic bomb blasts on personality? We cannot.

A variety of research strategies is available. Which one the investigator selects is at least partly determined by the research question. Experimental and correlational research are the two major forms of research distinguished by most psychologists. Some who write about the topic label all nonexperimental, nonmanipulative research as correlational. Others restrict the meaning of correlational research more and have classification schemes including other research strategies, such as the case history method and the survey method. However, for our purposes, a crucial distinction hinges on whether or not the investigator manipulates the subject's environment in some way.

SOME OTHER ISSUES IN RESEARCH

 e have already said that behavior is terribly complex. We will develop that point further. We will discuss the interrelatedness of questions—an interrelatedness that has, paradoxically, led psychologists to attempt to develop progressively less comprehensive theories. And, assuming that you may ask why we try to theorize at all, we will give you some of the reasons for theory construction. Also, we will attempt to present the position of those psychologists who adopt a radically different strategy. Let us now begin with the question of interrelatedness.

Interrelatedness of Questions

We have repeatedly indicated that nonresearchers ask numerous interesting and important questions that are scientifically unanswerable. Also many questions, although they sound scientific, are unanswerable in the terms in which they are asked. For example, What is the relationship between learning and perception? Does motivation affect learning? Does motivation affect perception? Does perception affect motivation? Does frustration necessarily lead to aggression? How do parental attitudes affect the later adult personality of a child?

Many of the reasons such questions cannot be answered scientifically were discussed in Parts I and II. But another difficulty may not be so apparent:

The complete scientific answer to any one of these grand questions about behavior is dependent upon our having complete answers to every other grand question about behavior.

In addition to all of the problems that were dealt with by reducing the question to manageable proportions, we also have the problem of the interrelatedness of the questions prior to any reduction. This interrelatedness has been recognized by every investigator cited in Part II. They held constant all possible influences on behavior except the one under investigation. Recall our discussion of control. Why did the various investigators go to such great pains to hold constant all extraneous influences? Why did they take what may have seemed to be such elaborate precautions? These precautions are eloquent testimony to the fact that these investigators were aware of all of the things that may, and do, affect behavior. One cannot study everything at the same time. So the researcher purposely ignores many things that would affect the results—ignoring them by holding them constant. But ignoring them in an experiment does not make them any less influential in real life. Holding these influences constant in an experiment does not mean that they are constant in real life. In fact, the many influences on behavior are interdependent; the effect of one may depend heavily on any number of others. For example, when an investigator chooses to study learning and selects adults as subjects, it is not because he or she believes that developmental considerations are irrelevant. It is because only so much can be studied at a given time. The fact that the developmental level is held constant does not mean that it is unimportant. It means that the investigator does not get any information about developmental influence or about the relationship between development and learning. But the investigator does get some information about the learning process in adults. Obviously this means that the *generalizability* of the research findings is limited. We will be dealing with this important issue of generalizability in detail in a later section.

We began with a question about stress and personality. But you may well have noticed that the studies presented in Part II dealt with diverse topics: developmental and social psychology, psychosomatic illness, learning, perception, abnormal behavior and its treatment, and so on. It may seem that this was possible only because the construct *personality* refers to the whole person; but, in fact, the same could have been done for every one of the grand questions we posed. Consider what would be involved in establishing the relationship between motivation and learning. In order to investigate the problem scientifically, we would have to take all of the steps involved in reducing this complex relationship to answerable questions. But we also face the problem just raised in this section. In order to understand an individual's motivation, we must understand how the individual perceives the motivating situation. In order to understand the individual's perceptual process, we must understand the individual's past history, which requires an understanding of the developmental process, attention, learning, and memory. All of this implies an understanding of individual differences, as determined by biological and physiological considerations, along with the person's past history. Thus as the relationship between motivation and learning, for example, may well differ from individual to individual, any complete theory must deal with the problem of individual differences. This requires an understanding of different kinds of abnormal behavior as well as of different kinds of normal functioning. Thus the complete, scientific answer to any general question about behavior requires the complete, scientific answer to every other general question.

At the very outset of this book we said that virtually all "psychologists have now abandoned the pursuit of the Holy Grail of grand behavior theory." At least they have done so to the extent that they are not trying to construct such theories with the data at hand, nor are they trying to obtain the data that will lead to a grand theory in the foreseeable future. Everything you have read between the two writings of that phrase contributes to an explanation of why this pursuit has been abandoned. An investigator who wishes to provide a complete answer to a grand question about behavior is faced with the task of reducing the question to a large number of answerable ones. The investigator is also faced with the presently impossible task of understanding all related aspects of behavior, that is, all of behavior.

There is another reason why grand theorizing has become a thing of the past. If we judge the value of a theory in terms of its capacity to predict events with greater simplicity and accuracy than competing theories, this problem comes sharply into focus. Many grand theories simply could not predict the great bulk of behavior in any specific way. Yet once *any* given behavior occurred, the theory could easily "explain" what happened and why. But so could the competing theories! Such successful *postdiction* is often mistakenly interpreted as sufficient evidence that a theory is correct. In those limited areas in which a grand theory could predict some specific behaviors and thus appear to have value, these same specific predictions could have been made by the competing grand theories. Thus the data (the fact that predictions came true) provided no conclusive evidence for the value of one grand theory over another.

There was a time in psychology when a tremendous amount of research effort was expended in attempts to demonstrate that one grand theory was better than another, that it was more correct and accurate in predicting the outcome of research. Experiments were constructed by proponents of theory A to show "once and for all" that theory A was right and theory B was wrong. Unfortunately, once the data came in, proponents of theory B could incorporate the results as easily as could those of theory A. Thus neither theory really gained in terms of its explanatory power or its status as a scientific theory. Partly because of multitudes of such experiments and such outcomes, the era of the "crucial experiment" has passed, along with the era of grand behavior theory.

The above helps to explain why many psychologists are trying to construct much smaller theories, covering only a very limited range of behavior. For example, some psychologists are trying to construct theories to explain how retarded children learn to differentiate between different but similar stimuli. Others are attempting to build miniature theories to explain color perception and color blindness. There are miniature theories of hearing that try to describe the processes by which sound waves are converted to nerve impulses. Many other such limited theories exist—theories of speech perception, short-term memory, self-perception, dreaming, and so forth.

The construction of such a miniature theory may be possible in the lifetime of a psychologist only because the psychologist has deliberately reduced its generality, thereby excluding many other phenomena. In experiments the psychologist controls these other phenomena, keeps them constant, and prevents them from having an effect.

Some psychologists strive for the development of good miniature theories in the anticipation that someday their limited theories will become parts of more comprehensive theories. Other psychologists pursue the goal of good miniature theories because they are convinced that the limited area they are trying to understand is important in and of itself. They believe that their efforts will contribute significantly to the understanding of behavior. Again this discussion touches on the whole issue of the generalizability of research.

Why Theory?

At this point, or perhaps earlier, you may have wondered, But why theory? If developing a comprehensive theory of behavior is as difficult a task as we have said, then why should we bother theorizing at all? The response to that question is very complicated.

Part of the answer lies in the history of science. By applying scientific theory, the physical sciences have been remarkably successful in understanding and controlling many aspects of the physical environment. Scientific theory has proven to be one of the most powerful tools the human race has ever employed. In the past couple of centuries the application of the scientific method in fields like physics, chemistry, and agriculture has led to an astonishing improvement in our physical environment. No comparable improvement has been forthcoming in our social environment or in our understanding of behavior. Because of the success brought about in other fields by scientific theory, many psychologists believe that the theoretical approach will be profitable for the behavioral sciences as well. They argue that a good theory will be a significant contribution to the understanding of behavior.

There is another part of the answer to the question, Why theory? but before we can present it meaningfully, we have to discuss briefly the nature of scientific theory.

Scientific theory is generally regarded as a means of bringing order to the available knowledge about the universe. Theories essentially involve some broad assumptions (e.g., people can be studied as a physical energy system), a set of interrelated constructs, such as we have discussed above, and rules for relating the assumptions and the constructs to observables. The value of a scientific theory depends in part upon the extent to which it orders knowledge. Frequently it is possible to construct two theories of roughly equal simplicity, both of which explain the same set of data, the same experiments, and the same body of knowledge. One of these theories may be rich in suggesting new hypotheses and new experiments and may lead to a considerable amount of new knowledge. To the extent that it does this better than the alternative theory, it is the better, more general theory. There are other ways of evaluating a scientific theory. One of these was implied a few sentences above with the expression, "of roughly equal simplicity." That is, a good theory should explain a large number of facts with relatively few assumptions and constructs. Ideally, a theory should be so explicit that testable hypotheses can be logically deduced from it.

Given this very brief discussion of the nature of theory, let us now come back to the question posed earlier, Why theory?

The second part of the answer to that question really reflects the psychology of scientific investigators. There is an intrinsic reward in constructing a good theory, even a very limited theory. Theorists who weave together ideas in such a way that they can now integrate a set of facts which had previously seemed unrelated and, indeed, predict new facts experience a great personal satisfaction. Part of it involves a belief that one has contributed to the advancement of the science. But there is more to it than that. There is a sense of excitement and the exhilaration of discovery—at least for the successful theorists. In the best of circumstances, the process is a self-replenishing, self-sustaining one. The data of new investigations require modification of the theory, and perhaps open up novel lines of research requiring yet further modification. We can't communicate the satisfaction involved in creating a good theory. It comes from many sources, not the least of which is the experience of success in a task that a person believes both difficult and important.

However, some psychologists say that theory construction is not, at the present time, the best approach to take. They argue that at the present stage of development of the science, psychology is not ready for the construction of theories of behavior. When they say that psychology is not ready, what do they mean? They mean that even with the great amount of research carried out in the past few years, psychologists simply have not been exploring behavior fruitfully. They argue that we have wasted time and effort asking the wrong questions. Psychologists who have been developing theories have been trying to gain some understanding of behavior by postulating constructs— anxiety, emotion, arousal, fear, the unconscious, stress, personality. It can be argued that a good deal of research time and energy has gone into studying behavior in an effort to clarify the nature of our constructs rather than studying behavior in an effort to predict and control that particular behavior. In fact, we must carry out many studies relating to a construct before that construct can be useful—before we can employ it to understand behavior in a wide variety of settings. We must be able to show through research that by using a construct like conflict we are better able to understand behaviors that may seem unrelated. *No theoretical construct can be defined or made useful in the above sense by carrying out only one experiment.*

Psychologists in the tradition of B. F. Skinner have argued that these constructs not only are unnecessary for our understanding of human behavior but may actually interfere with such understanding. They argue that we don't need constructs and that we don't need all of these complex theories. If they are right, we don't need to carry out all of this research that focuses upon constructs and theories. The Skinnerians have an alternative. They argue that we can understand behavior through a careful analysis of the *contingencies* in the environment. By contingencies, they are referring primarily to the consequences of the response an organism makes and to the stimuli in the environment that inform the organism about what those consequences will be, thereby controlling the behavior. Let us consider a concrete example.

Suppose we put a food-deprived pigeon in a chamber that contains a key which the bird can peck. Also suppose that each time the animal pecks the key a bit of food is delivered (that is, the consequence of the pecking response is food delivery). Soon we would have the bird shaped so that whenever we deprived it of food and placed it in the chamber, it would peck the key and eat. Getting food is contingent upon the pigeon's pecking the key. The result is that each time the pigeon pecks and receives food, the probability that it will peck again in the same situation is increased. We could then put a red light over the key and set up the apparatus so that no matter how many times the pigeon pecked, it would not receive food unless pecking occurred with the light on. In time the red light would become one of the stimuli that control the response; that is, the bird would not peck unless the light were on. As far as the Skinnerians are concerned, we now have everything necessary to understand the pigeon's behavior. We can predict the bird's behavior from a knowledge of the stimuli in its environment and a knowledge of its history in that environment. We can predict the pigeon's behavior and we can control it. If it is deprived of food, the pigeon will peck the key when the red light is on. If we turn the red light off, it will stop pecking. We know this because we know what the environmental contingencies regarding pecking and receiving food have been; we know what the relationships have been between the red light, the pecking responses, and the presentation of food. The Skinnerian is able to point to the relationship between antecedent conditions and consequent behaviors. The bird has been deprived. Pecking has led to food delivery. Is it necessary to know any more? Notice, no reference has been made to constructs, not even to hunger drive! No assumptions have been made about what intervenes between the antecedent condition and the consequent behavior.

Within this framework the understanding of behavior simply refers to our ability to specify the observable conditions under which a response will occur. If you think back to the section on Dicky, you will recall that Wolf, Risley, and Mees were simply interested in shaping and controlling the boy's behavior by manipulating his environment, much as the pigeon's behavior in the chamber was shaped and controlled. They referred to no "emotions" or "personality constructs."

The case of Dicky provides a good contrast between the highly theoretical approach to understanding behavior and the approach taken in the Skinnerian tradition. One could ask the question, How can we explain Dicky's tantrums? The theoretically oriented psychologist could well invoke a number of constructs to explain the behavior disturbances observed and argue that the boy's self-destructive behaviors were symptoms of an underlying disorder which caused hostility toward his parents. Or it could be argued that Dicky was suffering from strong feelings of rejection, causing him to behave in ways that would call attention to himself. Similarly one could invoke concepts, such as conflict or frustration, to explain the tantrums and the glasses-throwing. In fact, since Dicky suffered a severe visual impairment, it could quite easily be argued that he was constantly frustrated since he could not see clearly and thus could not easily interpret the events in his environment. In fact, constructs like these are often used when psychologists attempt to "diagnose" or understand the behavior of others. But let us contrast this with the Skinnerian position that these constructs are just not useful in predicting and controlling behavior. To Skinnerian psychologists the important facts have nothing to do with what is going on inside people. They would argue that all we need to do is specify the behavior we want to predict and control, determine the contingencies related to it, and change the behavior by manipulating those contingencies.

Results like those obtained with Dicky are pointed to as strong evidence for this position. Yet many other psychologists view such outcomes differently. Recall that before Dicky was seen by Wolf, Risley, and Mees, he had been variously diagnosed as mentally defective and schizophrenic. Regardless of the label, it was generally agreed that Dicky had very severe problems in adjustment. Wolf, Risley, and Mees were able to *shape* certain behaviors and eliminate tantrums and glasses-throwing, but they did not "cure" Dicky.

Psychologists would still consider Dicky's general adjustment to be abnormal even though he may now wear glasses and not have tantrums. While the gains made were important, they were also very limited. For example, despite the fact that attempts were made to improve the boy's verbal behavior, Wolf, Risley, and Mees state: "His verbal behavior is by no means comparable to that of a normal five-year-old child" (p. 311). Outcomes like this are often generally the case whenever the Skinnerian approach is applied to such severe behavior problems. Critics of this approach argue that just as only a small segment of Dicky's behavior was modified, so also this entire mode of attack, while successful, is drastically limited (DesLauriers & Carlson, 1969). This is not to say that working on highly specific, restricted behaviors is unimportant. Consider the work of Budzynski and his colleagues on tension headaches. They dealt with a highly restricted behavior, tension at a particular muscle site that presumably caused a specific kind of headache. They were exceedingly careful to ensure that they had a particular kind of patient who suffered a specific kind of headache—patients who did not suffer from other emotional problems. But consider an essential difference between Dicky and the headache patients. In Dicky's case the specific behaviors that were changed (i.e., tantrums and the glasses-throwing) were important, *but* they were not the central problem the youngster faced. The manipulations changed certain overt behaviors and changed them for the better. Yet Dicky remained an abnormal child. In the case of the headache patients the tension headaches were the problem. Once these specific problems were eliminated, the immediate reason for obtaining help was also eliminated.

We do not wish to give you the impression that the differences between the theoretical approach and the Skinnerian tradition occur only in the area of clinical psychology. Skinnerians raise the very same objections to theoretical approaches in every area of psychological research. They object to explanations of the phenomena of learning, perception, and motivation that rely on unobservables. They argue that more progress would have been made in psychology had we spent our time describing functional relationships—that is, systematically categorizing the relationships between antecedent conditions, behavior, and the consequences of that behavior.

We don't want to imply that psychologists who reject the strategy of theoretically oriented research are necessarily "Skinnerians." Many researchers study behavioral events without attempting to build theories or to develop and validate constructs, yet they still do not subscribe to the major Skinnerian premises. That is, they do not believe that behavior is solely a function of environmental antecedents and environmental consequences.

By now you may have asked yourself, After all these years of research haven't psychologists been able to find out which of these strategies is better? Don't they know yet if we can learn more about behavior by doing theoretical research or by rejecting such an approach? The answer to the question of which approach is better is simply not available given the current status of psychology. It may never be available.

There is another important distinction to be made, similar to the theoretical-atheoretical distinction we have been discussing. That is the distinction between basic and applied research. *Basic research*, also called pure research, involves the search for knowledge essentially for its own sake, while *applied research* involves the search for knowledge that is relevant to some particular problem, some particular practical application. While the distinction seems roughly analogous to the theoretical-atheoretical one, basic research may well be either theoretically oriented or based on a hunch! Similarly, applied research may be theory-directed, or it may be an all-out attempt to find out whatever works, without regard to theoretical considerations at all. Note, however, that while the basic and applied behavioral scientists may be motivated by different interests, their methods are fundamentally the same, involving objective observations, control, and very often quantification.

Ethical Considerations

The word *ethics* implies a set of rules regarding how people "ought" to behave, rules differentiating right from wrong. Science has little to tell us about ethics. Scientific investigations provide data about the way the world *is*, but they do not answer questions about the moral or ethical goodness of that state of the world. For example, the social scientist may be able to provide data regarding how many people *do* believe in a supernatural being, but these data cannot tell us if this belief is "good" or "bad."

Do not be misled by the above into thinking that scientists are not concerned with ethical questions. As people and as professionals, many scientists are deeply concerned about ethical issues. Ethical issues involve concerns raised by the specific operations employed in research and in clinical practice. They also involve the use—or misuse—of scientific knowledge. Let us examine some specific areas in which psychologists are concerned with ethical principles.

We have seen that for many reasons psychologists use animals as research subjects. As we have often pointed out, methodological considerations and convenience are reasons for using such subjects. But in many cases animals are used because of ethical considerations. Consider Brady's work on ulcer formation. The major index of change was physical damage to the organism. Brady was *trying* to produce physiological damage in an effort to understand ulcer formation in humans. In fact, he stressed the animals so severely that they died. Obviously, manipulations having such drastic outcomes cannot be carried out on people. This is not to say that we cannot investigate ulcers in humans. We can study ulcer patients in many ways. We can give them psychological and physiological tests to determine how they differ from people who don't have ulcers. We can study the family or social backgrounds of ulcer patients to see if these backgrounds differ from those of nonulcerated persons. What we *cannot* do is place healthy individuals in stress situations aimed at *producing* ulcers. If we wish to investigate the immediate conditions leading to ulcers under controlled conditions, the only way to do it is to manipulate the factors we think lead to ulceration and observe the outcome. In this case the only choice is to use animals as subjects. Many of the studies presented in Part II of this text were aimed at answering questions that could be ethically answered only with animal subjects.

The discussion so far must have led you to wonder if we are at all concerned with the humane treatment of animals. The answer is Yes. Very specific ethical standards govern the care and treatment of research animals. These standards require proper physical care of animal subjects. It is ethical to sacrifice animals, but it is unethical to do so in a way that causes them to suffer unduly. When research animals undergo pain or must be sacrificed, it is because this is the only way the information may be obtained. Even then, it is permissible only when the investigator has some real chance of discovering something meaningful. For example, Masserman produced some rather severe behavior disorders in his cats. He was attempting to understand the conditions leading to the suffering involved in human neurosis. The expectation that he might answer significant questions concerning these conditions was reason enough to carry out his research.

The problems with human subjects are far more complicated. Clearly, manipulations that might lead to lasting damage must never be used. But what about experiments that might cause the subject some minor pain, discomfort, or some loss of self-esteem? Should they be done? One consideration relevant to this question involves the principle of informed consent, which means that the potential subject must be told what is going to happen and be given the choice to participate or not. For example, when painful stimuli are to be used, subjects are told this and not required to participate. When Johnson studied psychophysiological responses to stress, he used only volunteers who experienced a sample shock before they agreed to participate.

Ethical considerations not only rule out any procedures that may lead to permanent harm but also require researchers to make certain that any negative effects of their operations are eliminated. Consider Johnson's research again. In the case of both the difficult and the impossible discrimination groups, the last few trials were made easy for the subjects. Thus they got them right, avoided shock, and likely left the experiment considerably less upset than they might have been.

But again the problem is much more complicated. Consider Schachter's investigation into affiliation. It would have been impossible to do that research if he had explained what he was going to do ahead of time. He not only did not inform his subjects of the nature of the research in which they were about to participate, he deliberately deceived them. In order to induce anxiety he told some subjects they would receive painful shocks. But they received none! Schachter had to explain to them after the experiment why they had been deceived and what the real purpose of the experiment was; that is, he *debriefed* them. For the most part, psychologists don't deceive subjects without carefully considering alternative methods of answering the question. If researchers can perform a relevant experiment without deception, they do. If they cannot, they must decide if the question they are answering is important enough to warrant the operations. There are psychologists who believe that the profession has not gone far enough to protect the public. They argue that too many potentially harmful experiments have been done without any "real chance of discovering something meaningful." They argue that deception is so widely practiced that the major result is not meaningful knowledge but widespread cynicism about psychological research. You should think about the ethical implications of the experiments you read about earlier in this book. The most fascinating experiments often raise the most profound problems. Two of the most widely publicized experiments in recent years asked questions of considerable social relevance and created a storm of controversy over ethical issues. Milgram (1974) led subjects to believe they were delivering intense shocks to other people. The other people were actually confederates of Milgram. Did his debriefing repair the damage to the subjects' self-esteem? Was the knowledge gained about the conformity and obedience displayed by the subjects worth the cost to the subject? Milgram's ethical judgment came down on the side of doing the experiment. Many other psychologists agree with him. Many do not. You will very likely read about Milgram's experiment in the social psychology section of your text. What is your judgment? Don't permit yourself the luxury of a quick, easy answer. Similarly, you will also likely read about the second experiment, the Stanford prison study by Philip Zimbardo and his colleagues (Haney, Banks, & Zimbardo, 1973). In that experiment students played the roles of prisoners and guards. Their behaviors changed profoundly. Could their prior consent, which the experimenter obtained, possibly have been "informed"? Even the experimenters were taken by surprise by what was happening, and they terminated the experiment early. Was the knowledge worth the cost to the students? To the profession? Zimbardo's answer was Yes. Again, other psychologists disagree. *You* think it through when you read about that research. Perhaps in the long run the knowledge gained from these two experiments will influence a large number of people and will inoculate them against behaving in such conforming ways.

The issues so far discussed relate primarily to the ethics of research. The issues become even more complex when dealing with those psychologists who are trying to help. Consider those who work with disturbed people. These professionals must also follow ethical guidelines in applying clinical techniques. Recall the work that Wolf, Risley, and Mees did with Dicky. They brought certain aspects of his behavior under their control by shaping his responses much as we do with animals in the laboratory. In fact, these psychologists went so far as to deprive the boy of food! You may have wondered if such operations are ethical. Consider the situation. Wolf, Risley, and Mees faced a decision. Dicky would lose his vision. They had to do something to help him. But what? They knew that food deprivation is a potent source of motivation. But taking food away from a child is a drastic act. They had to decide which was worse for Dicky, going blind or going hungry. Dicky had nothing to say about it. They had to make an ethical as well as a clinical judgment. Going hungry for a short period of time seems to us to have been a very small price for Dicky to have paid for his vision. However, the ethical questions that therapists face are not always so easily decided.

The work with Dicky exemplifies a broad ethical issue that all psychologists who actively intervene in the life of another human being must face. The psychologist must ask the question, Should I change this person's behavior? or (perhaps even more to the point), Is the behavior I want to substitute for the maladaptive behavior really better?

Of course, another question can also be raised, Do psychologists who believe they have the knowledge and skill needed to help a person have the right *not* to help? This question is especially critical for the psychologist who is trying to investigate the worth of some form of therapy. Consider the biofeedback research discussed in Part II. Budzynski and his colleagues chose an experimental approach to investigate whether biofeedback might reduce tension headaches. In order to carry out the research plan, the experimenter-clinicians administered the biofeedback treatment to a group of subjects; but they also had a control group, a group that had tension headaches but whose function in the experiment required that they *not* be treated. Budzynski and his colleagues met their ethical problem head-on by offering treatment to all of the control subjects immediately after the termination of their experiment. In other investigations, especially those involving long-term treatments, the ethical dilemma is not so easily resolved.

Other practitioners are trying to come to terms with equally profound ethical issues. Certainly the psychologists who work with psychological testing are facing large issues, especially with respect to questions of discrimination in tests that are used in decisions about hiring or for entrance to a university or professional school.

How do we resolve ethical problems? *There are no simple solutions.* No general code of ethics will nicely resolve the problems researchers or practitioners face in an actual situation. This is true no matter how useful this code may sound.

Where Do the Questions Come From?

We have written much about how researchers go about the business of answering questions. However, we have not addressed ourselves directly to the issue of where questions come from. There are innumerable sources.

A major source of questions is theories about behavior. One of the basic requirements of any theoretical system is that its propositions can be tested. Some questions are derived directly from a theory and represent attempts to confirm the theory. Hunt's research is an example of a question derived from a theory. Ideally, research like this is intimately tied to the constant development and modification of our theories of behavior.

A second common source of questions is the research process itself. Many researchers believe that one criterion for a good study is the number of new questions it raises. Experimenters generally carry out a piece of research to answer a specific question. They may get their answer, but often the results suggest many other questions, which may or may not be related to the original question. Perhaps while observing the behavior of their subjects, they may discover an experimental manipulation that they had not even considered. Or perhaps the results will be so different from what the experimenters expected that they cannot be understood without further research. The failure to replicate previous research might lead to further experimentation so that the conflicting results can be understood. Thus the data from any one experiment can be the stimulus for a program or even a lifetime of research.

Sometimes researchers approach a particular question but discover that they cannot construct an experiment to answer it. Very often this is because no one has developed a methodological technique or a particular measurement procedure needed for the research. These situations give rise to many questions that, in and of themselves, require research to answer. Thus it is not unusual to find psychologists doing large-scale studies simply to answer questions about techniques that they then apply to their original research question.

Much research is carried out in an effort to answer practical questions. Questions like, How can we select the best of a large number of applicants for a job? often lead psychologists to carry out massive research programs to construct appropriate psychological tests (recall the development of the test for success in pilot training). Psychologists also carry out a great deal of research stimulated by practical clinical problems. For example, we try to construct tests that will tell us if a mental patient is a suicide risk. We investigate psychotherapy techniques to determine the best way to treat certain types of emotional disorders. These kinds of questions are often approached with a minimum, if any, interest in theoretical considerations. Rather, a problem "out there" demands an answer. The question really comes from practical concerns of people in the community who are trying to get an answer to immediate, real-life questions. Wolf, Risley, and Mees' work with Dicky and the work on systematic desensitization of phobic patients exemplifies to some extent this kind of an approach. The research on sensory deprivation previously described also illustrates research stimulated by a practical, socially significant problem.

The sources of questions so far discussed are related either to practical problems or to already existing theory and research. However, many questions are derived from much less logical sources. Let's consider some of these.

Many times a psychologist who has been reading the results of other people's research may say, "These findings are interesting. I wonder what would happen if . . . ." The "if" means if I did an experiment investigating some previously unexplored relationships. Chances are the idea has not come from any serious consideration of theory. It may, in fact, come from a hunch. Schachter's work on affiliation is an example of a research project stimulated by a hunch or by intuitive reasons. This is not to say the ideas, once formalized, are less well thought through or less well developed. It is to say, however, that questions often result when a scientist sits around and talks, thinks, or argues with colleagues or students.

Another source from which questions arise is simple curiosity about the events occurring around us. Many human behaviors are just plain interesting but not understood. A researcher may simply begin with the question, I wonder what that's all about? or the statement, That doesn't make sense to me. Perhaps this is the very process that Cannon went through before he undertook his research on voodoo death.

The concept of luck is not a very scientific notion although everyone recognizes that sometimes fortuitous events may even shape history. So it is with science. Many times what turn out to be important scientific questions result from totally unexpected sources. Recall Brady's ulcer research. He and his colleagues were not looking for ulcers in their monkeys. They didn't expect them to die. But one did. And they found an ulcer. This unexpected result stimulated Brady and his colleagues to begin a whole new research program. Questions about ulcer formation and shock avoidance immediately became apparent, and since then a number of experiments in the area have been carried out by various investigators. Similarly, B. F. Skinner (1959) reports that early in his career an apparatus failure led him to an understanding of the effects of not rewarding rats for making previously learned responses. That led to a great deal of further research.

We have discussed several sources of scientific questions. There are certainly many more. You should recognize that the various sources outlined above are not really as independent as has been implied. Good hunches come in part from a solid understanding of the content of psychology and the methods of science. Also, questions arising from previous work often include theoretical interpretations. Many times it is difficult to specify the exact source of any one question, and we have not attempted to categorize each of the examples in Part II. The point is, *Questions can come from anywhere.* There are no rules and no restrictions regarding where the scientist gets ideas. The rules relate to how the question is asked and answered.

We have indicated a couple of times that we would return to the question of generalizability of research findings. Understanding of this and related issues is crucial to your ability to read about, interpret, and assess the value of psychological research. Thus the purpose of the next section is to discuss some of the issues that influence the generalizations that can be made from the kinds of studies we have described in Part II.

GENERALIZABILITY

To generalize means to infer a general principle that goes beyond the results obtained. Generalizations may refer to a larger group than the group studied, manipulations *like* the ones used, measures *like* the ones taken, or all of the above! As we said at the outset of this book, beginning students often think of the scientific psychologist as doing research that attempts to provide answers to very important, very general, grand questions. However, we have been saying all along that those questions must be rephrased. They must be cast into what may seem to be not only less general but also less "interesting," less "exciting," and less "important" terms. But the very process of rephrasing our questions into terms that allow objective observation and experimental control means those questions are answered under limited, highly specific conditions. Can we get back to the grand question? Can we take findings from laboratory experiments or from controlled observations of narrowly selected aspects of behavior and make inferences about behavior in the real world? To put the question in a nutshell, *How generalizable are our research findings?* It is this basic issue of generalizability that gives rise to the title of Section III of this book.

Do not confuse this issue with the immediate usefulness or applicability of the answers, which is the issue of applied versus basic research. The present issue involves a much broader question, Are we currently doing research in a way that will eventually lead us to understand human behavior *outside* the laboratories and other specific settings in which the research is done?

The historical development of psychology as a science cannot be outlined here. But one point is extremely important for what follows. Early in the development of psychology, researchers largely adopted the experimental model that had proven so successful in the physical sciences (see, for example, papers by Deese, Joynson, reprinted in Marx & Goodson, 1976). That is, psychologists in large measure adopted the basic approach to the discovery of knowledge that involves the experimental study of the "pure" case. If experimenters are interested in the influence of A on some behavior, they take A out of its real world context into a laboratory and "purify" it by holding B, C, D, etc., constant while manipulating A and observing the behavior. We have emphasized this approach in this book. The experimental method has worked spectacularly well in the physical sciences. Laws of optics carefully worked out under controlled conditions led to a fuller understanding of the world, and to significant applications in the world, because the laws describing the behavior of light are mightily robust! By robust, we mean that light behaves the same way under very different conditions, whether in a laboratory or in your home. But what about the behavior of people? Do people behave the same way under very different conditions? Can we take people into a laboratory and expect selected aspects of their behavior to be anything like those aspects outside the laboratory? Can we hold B, C, D, etc., constant, and have A's influence on behavior not be changed in some fundamental way?

Psychologists followed the lead of the physical scientists in the hope that psychological findings from controlled laboratory settings would *generalize* to the uncontrolled natural environment. How well is this hope being fulfilled? Nobody can answer this with certainty. Nevertheless, it is extremely important for the student of psychology to be aware of the issues involved in the question. They are complex and intertwined. We will discuss generalizability from the point of view of four basic topics: (1) subjects, (2) appropriateness of manipulations and measurements, (3) controls, and (4) replication.

Subjects

The behavior of animals has always had a fascination for people. Some research psychologists are interested in animal behavior, just as some biologists are interested in trees, and geologists in rocks. If, for example, a psychologist wishes to understand how wolves establish and maintain territoriality, then that psychologist should study wolves. But what about the many psychologists whose ultimate interest is in understanding human behavior? Should such psychologists study wolves? Or monkeys? Or rats? Or only people? That is a difficult issue. Why do many psychologists whose ultimate aim is understanding people spend so much time studying lower animals? We have already provided two answers to this question: (1) certain manipulations would be unethical with human subjects and (2) certain practical and methodological problems are most easily solved using animal subjects. The researcher is often in a bind and must either reduce the question about human behavior to a form that involves the use of animals or else drop the question. The ethical and practical reasons for using animals are compelling. But the fact that using animals is the only way to do the research does not address the critical question, What do the data mean regarding human behavior? That's what we will talk about now.

When we introduced the Brady section, we focused on the term "executive," noting that the term conjured up the image of a big boss handling big problems. The title of Brady's study, "Ulcers in 'Executive Monkeys,' " suggested these images. In some ways the experimental situation was analogous to the human executive's dilemma. But in an uncountable number of other ways it was *not* analogous. Masserman's work on experimental neurosis and his attempts to provide therapy for his disturbed cats were in some ways analogous to human conflict and to attempts psychologists make to help. But in many other ways they were not. Are the analogies close enough to allow us to make statements about people or to see human behavior in a new way because of our understanding of the animals' behavior? Or are the analogies really not close, and is their impact exaggerated by the titles of the studies and by the terms used to name the constructs and describe the operations? Do human beings really learn to fear previously neutral situations by the same process as Miller's rats? The use of animals involves the problem of generalizability across species but may also create other problems. The use of animals when we're interested in people may demand manipulations and measures that, while appropriate to the species being studied directly, may be different *to some unknown degree* from manipulations and measures appropriate to people.

It would be foolish for us or for you to assert that animal research is irrelevant to understanding human behavior, if that seems to be the implication of the above paragraphs. Renowned scientists have devoted their professional lives to studying behavior using animal subjects. They argue that there is a continuity of process across the species of the animal kingdom (to which humans belong) and that this continuity justifies the use of infrahuman subjects. That is, they argue that the learning process, for example, is fundamentally similar in some important ways in rats, in monkeys, and in people. But despite some continuity, rats are not people! Many processes are *not* the same. Irrespective of the carefully planned similarities of the animal experiment to a human situation, the innumerable differences between people and rats (or cats or monkeys or birds) seriously weaken even guarded claims to generalizability.

Many animal researchers also argue that while the results of animal studies do not directly generalize to human behavior, the data lead psychologists to a new understanding of complex relationships that can then be seen more easily in human behavior. This statement has a ring of truth to it, but there are difficulties with it, too. There is ample reason to believe that if you have a hypothesis you wish to prove in any area of research and you look at a rich enough source of data, you can find evidence confirming your hypothesis. Generalizing from animal research is no exception. The person who gets some hypothesis about people from animal research and then looks for evidence for that hypothesis in human behavior is almost *certain* to find some supportive evidence.

The use of animal subjects allows the investigator to use highly controlled, experimental situations and provides an aura of scientific respectability to psychological research. But there is a strong tendency for the investigator, or even more likely someone using the investigator's findings, to talk about the research results as though they mean much more than they do. Breger (1969), in discussing this issue, states that what many researchers assert is that " 'my approach is rigorous and scientific, I define my terms in a narrow operational sense; when I say anxiety I mean the response that the animal makes in this experimental situation.' Having established his claim to scientific status in this fashion, he then allows a host of meanings associated with terms such as anxiety and neuroses—meanings which his own definitions initially ruled out—to re-emerge and to bridge the gap from narrow experiment to broad application" (p. 39). Look back over Masserman's research and also at animal research presented in your text. See if you find this kind of *overgeneralization*.

The argument is not that researchers should lack precision in definition or that they should *not* do well-controlled studies. Rather the point is that generalizing the findings to human problems like "anxiety" and "neurosis" may not be valid. This is a strong statement. Breger makes basically the same point about learning:

Adopt, for a moment, the point of view of a naive but intelligent observer who knows nothing of the *reasons* psychologists give to explain their experiments. An investigator tells you he is interested in "learning" and you think to yourself: "This is certainly an important area with a direct bearing on all those years I spent in school learning, not to mention the learning that took place outside the classroom." You are then surprised to see that the investigator is not studying children at all but white rats. "All right," you think to yourself, "animals have to learn also, perhaps something of value can come from studying their simpler learning processes for, after all, biology has profited from the comparative study of animals." You are then again surprised to see that your investigator has no particular comparative interest and has, in fact, restricted his attention to the speed with which the rats can get through a maze and how this relates to sips of water or pellets of food or electric shocks that are given to them. You begin to wonder what possible relevance this enterprise can have for the learning that you experienced as a child. If you ask the investigator what his laboratory experiments have to do with school learning, he will give you a ready answer; you will, in fact, be treated to a brief lecture drawn from behaviorist ideology having to do with the place of rigorous experimentation in the development of scientific laws (or functional relationships) which, because of their objective character and extreme generality (like the law of gravity) have the most important relevance for the learning of almost anything by any organism in any situation. You will, in other words, be treated to a great deal of *argumentation* which attempts to prove that what is found out about how the sips of water or electric shocks affect the maze running performance of the rat does have relevance for the learning that human beings undergo. (1969, p. 40)

Even though Breger takes an extreme position on this issue, it is one that merits serious thought. However, as we have often said, you *must* ask, Where are the data? At this point no hard data demonstrate the *lack* of generalizability of results from animal studies to human behavior. On the other hand, no hard data exist suggesting such generalizability is warranted! Many psychologists believe that the payoff in understanding human behavior has not been great considering the enormous time and effort expended studying animals. Others disagree. The issue of generalizability has not been dealt with adequately in the psychological literature. The extent to which inferences from animals generalize to humans is itself at least partly answerable by research, but the way to go about doing the relevant research is unclear. Science is by tradition conservative, which means that the burden of proof is always on the investigator who claims new knowledge. In this case, it seems that the burden of proof is on the animal researcher who generalizes to human behavior, or on those writers who freely draw from animal research to explain human behavior.

The problem is not restricted to how well animal behavior parallels human behavior. Critics have charged that the data of psychology come primarily from investigations of white rats and college sophomores. The issue of generalizability across *human* populations is also an important one. To the extent that our research studies fail to demonstrate similar results with a wide range of human subjects, we cannot claim general laws of behavior. For example, Schachter's research on affiliation permits general statements about certain aspects of the affiliative tendencies of college women under stress. However, this single study does *not* tell us if a group of business executives, or a group of housewives, or a group of high-school students would behave in the same way. In order to find out, it is necessary to include these groups in the research.

As you read your introductory text, look carefully at the studies presented. Ask yourself the question, Has the author of the study or of the textbook attempted to generalize the findings beyond the reasonable limits of the subject population? Keep in mind that studies performed using college sophomores (or any other identifiable group) produce data that generalize to *similar* persons. Making statements that apply to people beyond the specific kind of sample studied is *overgeneralization*. It is speculation. Generalizability is not a property of a single study but of a large number of related investigations. However, be cautious in concluding that your textbook author may be guilty of overgeneralization. Textbooks often illustrate a general principle with a single study, but much more research has often been done related to the issue.

The question of generalizability is particularly relevant when a single subject is studied. Consider Silverman and Geer's work with the young woman's nightmares and phobia about crossing bridges. As we have indicated previously, this (and any single subject study) is limited because no control subject was used (i.e., a similar subject with a similar problem but who received no treatment). But the question for the present argument is, Given only one subject, is it reasonable to draw inferences about other subjects even though they may be highly similar in important ways? The answer is No! A sample size of one cannot be representative of any group or population of people. As useful as the single case study is, one such study by itself cannot produce knowledge that is directly generalizable to any other person or group of persons! Again, the demonstration of generalizability rests on a large number of related investigations rather than on the single study.

Manipulations and Measures

Recall the various research examples in Part II of this text. Think about the researcher's original questions; then think about how the terms of the questions were specified and reduced. You will remember this process of reduction as the development of the specific experimental manipulations to be employed and of the specific objective measures of behavior to be made.

Look at the studies in Part II and ask yourself, To what extent do the experimental manipulations and the observations made *sensibly* reflect the terms of the original question? Does telling college students they are going to receive electric shock produce an emotional state, "anxiety," that is the same as what we mean when we talk about "anxiety" in a person's life? Does simply moving closer to a caged, harmless snake after some brief "treatment" really provide a sufficiently close analog to important behavior changes in persons suffering from serious phobias?

Again, there is no simple answer. In thinking about generalizability, we ought to ask two related questions about the research we're concerned with. The first is, Has the interesting and important phenomenon asked about in the original question been so distorted by the process of reduction and redefinition of terms that it has been fundamentally changed? In other words, is the investigator now studying some behavior that he or she talks about *in the same words* as the original question but which no longer bears any sensible resemblance or relationship to that behavior as it occurs in nature?

The second, related question is, To what extent are the manipulations, measures, and results of any given experiment *sensible* in light of the manipulation, measures, and results of all other, related experiments? Ask yourself these questions as you read.

Control

We have repeatedly emphasized the concept of control. As you might guess, control and generalizability are related but in a complex and seemingly paradoxical way. Clearly, if a study is so poorly conceived that elementary controls are lacking, then no generalizations at all can be made from the results. The results would be meaningless. The apparent paradox is that when any single study is very highly controlled, the set of conditions to which the results generalize is small. If the behavior of the subject is highly predictable, but the subjects have been run in a very tightly controlled laboratory situation with nothing varying except that manipulation of interest, then to what situation can we generalize? We can generalize to conditions that are similar (or identical if you want to get hard-headed about it) to that tightly controlled laboratory situation. But, of course, nowhere in real life will you find that exact situation!

The question of generalization can be addressed in the same way as it was in the section on manipulations and measures. First, we must ask ourselves whether the investigator has fundamentally changed the question. That is, has the careful control changed the essence of the question by removing the manipulations and behavior from their natural context? If so, the original question is no longer being addressed. The new question is about some phenomenon created in the laboratory and perhaps existing only in the laboratory. For example, Neisser (1976) argues that this has happened all too often in perceptual and cognitive research. He writes, "If cognitive psychology commits itself too thoroughly to this model [using laboratory techniques to study a computer analogy to human behavior] there may be trouble ahead. Lacking in ecological validity, indifferent to culture, even missing some of the main features of perception and memory as they occur in ordinary life, such a psychology could become a narrow and uninteresting specialized field" (p. 7).

We must also ask whether a given experiment fits sensibly into the context of related investigations and just how broad that context of related investigations is. It is precisely here that the apparent paradox is resolved. If investigations with similar—but different—manipulations, measures, and controls continually come up with similar findings, then we have evidence for generalizability. We go beyond the data of an investigation, as we shall argue again shortly, when and only when data from other investigations make it sensible to do so.

Control is related to generalizability in yet another way. No matter how well controlled a particular study is, an investigator does not claim to have ruled out every possible event that could have produced the results. In fact, researchers don't try to study all of the possible events relating to any one aspect of behavior. For example, Masserman could not state that experimental neurosis is caused *only* by conflict. Perhaps sensory deprivation could also lead to neurotic behavior; perhaps the stress of having to make "executive decisions" could produce neurotic behavior. Masserman could not say, for he did not study these antecedents as they relate to experimental neurosis. He did, however, rule out events like experiencing an air blast or feeding frustration in the absence of conflict; he was able to say that these events which were *inherent* in his research did not, in and of themselves, produce experimental neurosis.

Hunt provides another example of the same point. As we have seen, he applied controls appropriate to asking the question, Does feeding frustration in infancy lead to adult hoarding behavior? But he cannot answer the question, Does experiencing electric shock in infancy lead to adult hoarding behavior? It may, but this latter question is irrelevant to Hunt's research. If he wanted to rule out shock as an important antecedent condition, he would have had to include in his study another group—a group that experienced shock.

Thus while we have repeatedly written that the purpose of control is to rule out alternative explanations of the results of an experiment, this statement is actually true in only a limited sense. Masserman's controls did not rule out sensory deprivation as a possible antecedent condition of experimental neurosis. He could not and did not control for *all possible* sources of influence on a particular aspect of behavior. This is not a criticism of Masserman. These comments apply generally to psychological research. No piece of research is a complete specification of all antecedent conditions leading to a particular behavioral change.

An important point is implicit in the above discussion. The basic assumption that an experimenter makes about behavior in general, and about the behavior under investigation in particular, determines the experimental manipulations and the control operations that will be employed. These assumptions, while enabling the experimenter to make sense out of some small aspect of behavior, drastically limit what can be observed. An investigator cannot obtain information about the potential influence of a condition that has been controlled because that influence has been kept constant—it cannot have an effect. Similarly, an investigator cannot obtain information about the potential effect of any number of other conditions that have not been included in the research. They simply weren't studied. The possible outcomes of a research project are considerably constrained by the initial beliefs, assumptions, and biases of the investigator.

It is important that you not come away from this discussion thinking that any lack of control is a fatal flaw, or even with the idea that lack of control necessarily implies a mistake by the investigator. This is yet another issue regarding controls and generalizability. We talked about a trade-off earlier in this book. Recall that the researchers who wanted to study the effects of systematic desensitization on a young woman's bridge phobia simply could not get adequate controls. When Balke, Hammond, and Meyer wanted to study conflict resolution, they couldn't either. Both studies lacked complete control, so did the work with Dicky, and so does a lot of other work. But in these and similar instances the lack of control is not an oversight. It does not reflect a poorly conceived study. Rather it reflects a trade-off—a trade-off between getting some data on an important question, no matter how tentative, and getting no data at all. Under certain circumstances— usually those in which we are trying to study behavior as it is occurring in the natural environment—it is impossible to have completely adequate controls. The researcher simply must do the best possible job of exercising control and then be cautious about the conclusions.

Replication

The question, Do results generalize? makes an implicit assumption that the results are reliable. That is, they are repeatable. Before accepting as fact a relationship some investigator finds and before attempting to generalize and integrate it with other facts, the investigator must know if the effect is real. By real we mean that the effect was not produced by chance. How do researchers go about determining the reliability of their findings? Most frequently they use some mathematical or statistical operations, which allow the investigator to determine if the findings could likely have been due to chance alone. If the probability of a result being due to chance is very low, then the effect is called *statistically significant* and is considered reliable. Notice that statistical significance does *not* mean socially or psychologically significant.

Despite the usefulness of statistical methods, it is important to realize a fundamental point: *No matter how statistically significant a finding is, the reliability of an effect can never be established with one study.* Reliability must be determined by *replication*. That is, the study must be done more than once with substantially the same result. This would be a true demonstration of reliability. But replication must be done with great pains to keep all of the important elements in the studies exactly the same (or as nearly exactly the same as is possible). Recall Johnson's study from Part II of this text. Many researchers have carried out this experiment using the same stimuli and the same response measures with college students. The results are the same from one laboratory to another. In fact, this finding is so reliable that the experiment is used in many universities as a laboratory demonstration.

Also recall Shurley's study on sensory isolation. The results of this work were interpreted in the context of other research and theory that at the time suggested such isolation was exceedingly stressful. In fact, many of his subjects undoubtedly *expected* the experience to be a highly aversive one. Reading the published excerpts from their reports, however, leaves the impression that the experience wasn't all that bad. (See the descriptions of the hallucinations beginning on p. 41 if you don't recall them.) For quite a while films and novels played up these results, using the power of this "brainwashing" technique as a dramatic device. However, subsequent replication of this work has led to a major reinterpretation of Shurley's findings. These subsequent studies have suggested that under the right conditions, the isolation experience might be *relaxing!* In fact, it has been suggested that such an experience may even be therapeutically beneficial (Suedfeld, 1975). Notice that the studies subsequent to Shurley's work were not failures to *replicate*. They were done generally in the same way, and people made similar responses. The difference is in how these reliable data are interpreted. We have given you two examples where research has been replicated. There are also instances where replication has been attempted and failed. That is, where researchers have essentially repeated the operations and measures of an experiment and have been unable to obtain the same results. For example, Miller and DiCara (1967) were able to show that under certain highly specified conditions rats could be taught to control their own heart rate "voluntarily." Given everything that was believed about the lack of voluntary control over heart rates, this was astonishing. However, after a considerable number of experiments by Miller and other researchers, Miller himself reported that the result was not reliable, that the finding could not be replicated (see Miller & Dworkin, 1974).

Keep in mind that researchers who claim to replicate must rigorously adhere to the idea that replication involves doing the exact study again with new subjects. Unless this is done, the research is not a replication. Recall the Brady study on ulcers in "executive" monkeys. To our knowledge, this study has never been replicated in the sense that other monkeys were put in the same experimental situation and the same outcome occurred. A number of studies have been referred to as failures to replicate (see Weiss, 1968). In this work not only were rats rather than monkeys used as subjects, but also the details of the method between the experiments differed. In general, the results of the rat studies were opposite to Brady's findings. Rats who could avoid shock ulcerated less than rats who could not. Consideration of the Weiss work as a replication of the Brady study has led some to conclusions that we consider inappropriate. For example, in discussing the differences in results between Brady and Weiss, Geen (1976) states that the Weiss findings are " . . . contrary to those of the executive monkey study [and] perhaps we should revise our ideas regarding the stress level of executives" (p. 81). Since the use of rats in the Weiss work precludes considering the studies as replication of Brady's work (a point Weiss himself raises), it does not make sense to consider the results as "contrary to Brady." Certainly the findings are different. They are opposite. But given the radical differences between the species of the subjects and the difference in the research designs, there is no reason to expect that the outcomes should necessarily be the same.

In thinking about the generalizability of the results of psychological research, the investigators should realize that a minimal criterion is necessary for the results to be reliable. Results can be considered reliable when the same findings emerge from studies that repeat the original operation.

Beyond Replication

As we said earlier, before we can ask the question of generalizability of an effect, we must demonstrate reliability. But reliability does not establish generalizability. In fact, to the extent that research is literally replicated (that is, same operations on similar subjects, etc.), we do not gain additional evidence for generalizability. What we have is evidence that under these specific conditions the observed result is repeatable.

To show generalizability investigators must be able to employ different kinds of operations and different kinds of measurements and still obtain the same results. When we say different kinds of operations and measurements, we mean different in a particular way. The operations and measurements may be physically different, but they must be psychologically equivalent. Recall that we discussed different methods of defining the same construct back in Part I. Ideally, the investigators should also be able to point to situations in which psychologically *non*equivalent manipulations and measures lead to *different* results.

Let's take an example from Part II. Think of Davidson's work on the systematic desensitization of snake phobias in college students. Continued exact replication of this study would be likely to show the effects are reliable. It would probably indicate that if we go through the exact same treatment and control operations, we would find that students who fear snakes and who receive systematic desensitization of a particular duration will come closer to a caged, harmless snake than would control group subjects. But this does not tell us about the generalizability of the systematic desensitization effect. For example, it does not tell us if systematic desensitization is effective with different kinds of fears. What is needed is research using different but equivalent operations (that is, different fears, different fear hierarchies, different measures of effectiveness, etc.). In fact, this is exactly what has happened. Recall that Silverman and Geer successfully treated a "bridge phobia." If you glance back at that study, you will see that they followed the general rules for systematic desensitization. But compare what they did to what was done in the Davidson study. You will see some real differences in the operations used in the two. Nevertheless, the treatment was successful. Also, many other researchers have shown similar effects with a wide range of specific fears. All of this evidence put together provides evidence for generalizability. However, there are limits to generalizability. Silverman and Geer provide no evidence that systematic desensitization operations will "cure" someone who has schizophrenia. There is evidence that systematic desensitization does not work as well with people who suffer from many different fears rather than one specific fear. This idea of limits upon generalizability is an important one. Research should be aimed at showing just how far we can generalize. The Weiss study is not, as noted above, a replication of Brady. But the different results are in themselves interesting. They demonstrate that we cannot make a generalization across species about the form of stress studied and its relation to ulceration.

We have tried to show you how important replication is and how important it is to go *beyond replication*. We could select a number of examples of both. However, we believe it is fair to say that psychologists have not gone far enough in these directions. There has been a very strong tendency for psychological researchers to go just *barely* beyond replication, to investigate some phenomenon in an almost unbelievably restricted range of conditions. The limits to which one can generalize are not set by the names we give the things we are studying (that is, anxiety, conflict, etc.). They are set by the range of conditions under which we actually obtain comparable results. Those conditions include subjects, manipulations, measures, and controls.

THINKING ABOUT BEHAVIOR

he above discussion emphasized the great difficulties involved in generalizing from psychological research. You should not mistake that discussion for a confession of despair. *It is not.* It is a recognition that the important task of understanding human behavior is very difficult and complicated.

Scientific psychology has established a number of generalizations about people, though not nearly as many as we would have liked or nearly as many as some who popularize psychology would have you believe. Among the things psychology has developed is a sounder body of knowledge than was previously available about the effects of reward and punishment on some forms of learning. We know, for example, that the effects of reward are much more predictable than those of punishment. For this and other reasons, reward is a much more effective means of controlling behavior in most situations. You might respond, "I knew that all along"; and you might cite folk wisdom to the effect that "you can catch more flies with honey than with vinegar." But folk wisdom also tells you that if you "spare the rod you'll spoil the child." In fact, a thorough enough search of recorded folk wisdom will tell you just about anything you want to know and also its opposite! Scientific psychology is also expanding our knowledge about some of the limitations on our capacities to think about things, especially limitations due to short-term memory. Certainly one product of scientific research into behavior has been the abandonment of many erroneous ideas about the sources of abnormal behavior.

Perhaps, though, the major appreciation you should carry away from this book is a recognition of our relative ignorance about human behavior. Most scientists who are engaged in research on some aspects of behavior are acutely aware of their *lack* of understanding, even of that area in which they specialize. But one thing we are beginning to know is how to think clearly about behavior. As scientists we know only too well when we do not fully understand some problem. The major skill we hope you will carry away from this book and from your course is an ability to *think more clearly about behavior*. Drawing on what you have read up to now, let's explore further how you might accomplish this. In order to set the stage for our discussion, we have to digress for a moment and report a hypothetical interview.

Suppose you turned on the TV and heard someone ask an "expert" in psychology some of those questions we listed back on page 2. A typical exchange might go something like this:

Q. How much influence does environment have on personality development?
A. Personality is definitely influenced in some ways by biological factors, but research shows that the major influences early in life are environmental—primarily the family; later on in life, peers are more important.
Q. What possesses a person to act like an authority about a subject even though he or she may know nothing about the subject?
A. Well, the person must know *something* about the subject to act like an authority, but I do understand the question, and it is a very good one. This kind of behavior usually reflects a deep-seated, even unconscious need for attention. People deprived of love and affection when they were younger are likely to show such a response pattern.
Q. Why are people prejudiced toward other people?
A. Well, one major reason is that when you put others down, you are building yourself up. It is a question of enhancing one's own self-esteem at the expense of others.

In order to place those answers in the perspective of this book, try to *reverse* the process we just went through in the discussion of generalizability. There we asked you to take an investigation and to ask what kinds of general statements can be made from the evidence. Now, take the above general statements and try to imagine what kinds of specific investigations would be needed to support the answers given by our "expert." What kinds of investigations, with all of the necessary reduction to observables, controls, and so on, would have had to be done in order to substantiate those answers scientifically? Those answers are generalizations. They ought to be based on data.

But they're not. They may sound like good answers. They have a certain aura of truth about them. They strike a responsive chord, especially when uttered by a multidegreed expert! But do they mean anything? In the first answer, personality is never even defined. Nor is anything else. Look at the second. Where are the definitions? Do you seriously believe that research evidence exists which would have established such a complex, long-term, causal relationship? Look at the third. Can you describe the research that would give you evidence for that answer? Does the answer really mean anything? Or is it somehow a rephrasing of the question? Does that third answer, that "explanation," refer to a general principle that makes sense out of behavior other than the specific behavior asked about? If not, it is not an explanation at all, but a verbal trick that no more answers the question than does a child who, when asked why, answers BECAUSE, THAT'S WHY! It is all too easy to get seduced by words, especially big words stated confidently by an authority. It is all too easy to accept a clever rephrasing of a question as an answer.

How might *you* develop the ability to think more critically about behavior? How might you learn to be able to think more critically, to recognize nonsense when you hear it, and to appreciate sound use of evidence when it is presented? That ability seems to us to be made up of two essential components. Those components feed and sustain one another in a reciprocal way. They are *knowledge* and a *questioning attitude*. We will develop each of these, describing the second component in terms of four key questions you should learn to ask.

Knowledge

In order to think clearly about any issue, you need knowledge. You need information. You need facts. Without facts you cannot think about an issue at all, much less think clearly about it. In your psychology course, you will learn many facts, including a sample of what research has been done, what the results were, and how different people have interpreted the results. You will learn also how they went about doing the research; that is, you will obtain a knowledge of how to go about "doing science." You will learn something about the major controversies in the field, which are not so much over the interpretation of single studies but are disagreements over broader conceptualizations of behavior.

Knowing the facts should enable you to recognize when a generalization is incorrect or perhaps when there is just not sufficient evidence to know if it is correct or not. Knowing the facts should help you identify unstated assumptions. To exemplify this latter point, just imagine hearing an explanation of behavior that uses Freudian terms as though they were unquestionably true. Knowing that there are alternative systems of thinking and that there are severe critics as well as strong supporters of the Freudian approach should enable you to recognize that the person talking is making a very large assumption—but not telling the audience. The assumption is that Freudian theory is correct.

The possession of knowledge will foster and interact with a questioning attitude. We referred to this attitude above; let us now focus on it. What kinds of questions should you ask when faced with either just plain uncertainty or with someone claiming to have an answer that leaves you wondering? Ask yourself,

What's the Question?

This is often a critical question to raise. Words, for all of their power, have different meanings to different people. This can create all sorts of confusion. As we showed in Part I, the careful definition of terms is essential to progress in scientific understanding. In trying to understand behavior, in evaluating answers to questions given in the media by "experts," or in communicating with others with whom you are trying to come to some common understanding, you should know what question you're really addressing. This is not always as easy as it may seem. Once the question itself becomes clear, you must also be concerned with whether a scientific attitude is appropriate. Ask yourself,

Can the Question Be Answered
by Reliance on Objective Observation?

In Part II we gave you examples of the use of objective observation to answer questions. But many questions simply cannot be approached that way. You would very likely agree with other people on whether a certain object is colored red. Whether you agree or not can be objectively observed. But do you "really see" and "really experience" the color red the same way other people do? That question cannot be addressed by using objective observations. A question about your (or anyone's) private experience cannot be answered scientifically.

Is capital punishment a just form of controlling crime? That, too, is a question that cannot be answered scientifically. Perhaps the question of whether or not capital punishment reduces the crime rate is reducible to questions for which objective observation will provide answers.

But that was not the question asked! The question asked was a question of value, a question of right and wrong. Many socially important questions involve both facts and values. One such question might be, What is the best way to raise children? Factual (and potentially scientific) components of the question include the effects of reward and punishment, the role of physical development, the role of imitation and identification, and many, many others. Value components include all of those aspects of the question that might be termed ends rather than means. You judge them as being right or wrong rather than as effective or ineffective. Whether or not you should try to develop in a child love of country and a sense of patriotism is primarily a value question. How you do it is a question of fact. The first cannot be addressed by scientific means. The second can.

The statement that a question cannot be answered scientifically does not mean that any answer is just as good as any other one. Questions of value must be subjected to clear, critical analysis in a fashion similar to questions of fact. The methods of answering such questions are different in some respects from the methods of science. The critical difference is that objective observations don't provide the answer. Questions of value are approached rationally, critically, carefully, but *subjectively.*

Once you have identified the question, or part of it, as being answerable by reliance on objective observation, then your attention can be focused on how to get the facts. Suppose you have concluded that objective observations are relevant to the question. Then you ask,

What Observations Can Be Made to Answer the Question?

Now you put yourself to the test! Do you really know what question you're asking? If so, you should be able to go and make the relevant observations in the world, in books, somewhere. Or else you should be able to conclude that while they could be made, you just can't do it (for reasons of time, money, personal limitations, etc.). If you are involved in some joint effort to get the facts, don't be surprised if you still disagree with the other investigators on what the obtained facts mean, even though you may agree on the facts. One of the most completely mistaken of folk sayings is "the facts speak for themselves." Facts, which are simply the agreed-upon results of objective observations, must be *interpreted.* Situations often arise in which different people (scientists included) in possession of the same facts come to very different conclusions. No matter how strongly you believe in some theory or explanation, you must realize that other beliefs, theories, or explanations might be just as consistent with the available evidence as is your theory. This brings us to the final question. Ask yourself,

Are There Alternative Explanations?

One thing that the scientist is supposed to do is to rule out alternative explanations of the data. The use of control in the experimental method does so automatically but only within the limitations discussed earlier. Recall that only certain kinds of alternative explanations are ruled out and also that competing theories in psychology were often able to "explain" the same behavioral data. One of the most significant effects of a good education is that an educated person can think about an issue from different perspectives. The educated person has more than one "model" of reality to help in thinking about people and things. You can develop alternative explanations, or understandings, of behavior from your psychology course. You can also do so by trying your best to understand events from other people's points of view. Certainly you should be reading your psychology text with the question constantly in mind, What assumptions must the person who made this statement be making? Some psychologists seem to take as a basic assumption—which in this context means simply an unstated part of the explanation—that people are "nothing but" input-output devices to be programmed to have a good life as defined by those who know how to do the programming. That sort of psychologist may be expected to behave quite differently in a position of influence (let us say in the administration of a school or of a prison) than one who believes that somehow people are ultimately responsible for their own lives.

You may be troubled and ask, Well, how do I figure out which explanation is right? How do I know the truth? Obviously, we have no simple answer to those questions. Human knowledge is highly tentative. The steps we take in looking for the truth are groping and sometimes blind. Hopefully, most of the steps in the scientific enterprise bring us "closer" to the truth (though many undoubtedly take us sideways). Again, we hope that after reading this book and taking your introductory psychology course, you will be at least able to recognize *nonsense* about behavior when you hear it. Suppose you went back and turned on the TV set again, and this time the talk show went something like this:

Q. Why does one's personality change under stress? How can psychologists help?

A. That's a pretty complicated question. Personality is something like a delicate tower of building blocks carefully arranged so that the integrity of the whole structure depends on the relations among the parts. The blocks include learning, motivation, attitudes, beliefs—all those things that go into the person's "makeup," those elements of the whole person, the personality structure. Well, stress is rather like someone pushing on the structure. The relationships among the parts get disturbed. The whole structure topples into disarray. The result is literally a breakdown—what lay people mistakenly call a nervous breakdown, but what we professionals term personality decompensation. How we can help depends, of course, on the individual. But basically we want to get people in distress to be open to others and to themselves. Openness to oneself leads to insight, and this insight provides the glue that helps hold the blocks together.

Now that sounds a great deal like a typical talk show explanation! But what does it mean? Any time the major premise of an explanation is an analogy, one that gives you a warm glow of understanding, try something. Put a *NOT* into the sentence. In the above case you get, "Personality is *not* something like a delicate tower of building blocks." That might give you an even warmer glow! It should make you reject the meaningless explanation given. It should make you look for better answers.

One assumption that underlies this book is that when dealing with the kinds of questions people ask about behavior,

There are no simple answers.
There are no simple solutions.

Next time you hear a politician say that the answer to violent crime is more punishment (lock 'em all up and throw away the key!), ask yourself what question is being asked about human behavior. What value considerations are involved? Ask yourself, What is the evidence? What assumptions are involved in the answer? Since the politician's solution obviously implies a generalization about crime, ask yourself if there are other possible explanations than what seems to be assumed. Ask also what other consequences would such an environmental manipulation have on society. But also ask yourself the same questions when you hear a social critic say that prisons should be closed because crime is not the fault of the criminal but is actually a symptom of a deeper sickness in society. What does it mean to say that society is "sick"? Anything? What does "fault" mean in this context? What are the consequences of the proposed action? Next time you hear an "expert" explaining what must have driven a mass murderer to commit such an unspeakable crime, be skeptical about the explanation—especially since such pronouncements are often made without the speaker having even *observed* the person, much less having observed the person *objectively*. The most extreme case of this is, of course, the psychological analysis of historical figures. If it's so easy to explain events after they happen, why is it so hard to predict them before they do?

A strong caution is in order. When someone proposes an explanation of some events that *you* cannot explain, that does not mean that *their* explanation is correct. Consider the controversy over whether or not some very bizarre behaviors are caused by possession by the devil. The fact that you cannot explain all of the strange behaviors and experiences in terms of generally accepted scientific principles does not prove that devils can enter our bodies and make us do bizarre things. *Your admission of ignorance is by no means proof of somebody else's explanation.*

CONCLUDING COMMENTS

he statement that there are neither simple answers nor simple solutions does not imply that one ought to throw up one's hands and say that nothing can be done. Sometimes situations call for immediate action; then you must act. Perhaps we must often act in partial ignorance and use partial solutions. But we act.

Do not mistake our questioning of the generalizability of research results for despair. Do not misread our assertion that knowledge is tentative as saying that we know nothing. Do not misunderstand the divergent philosophies and methodologies of psychological research as reflecting helpless confusion. Psychology is an *alive, vigorous* discipline. Disputes and differences reflect health, not sickness; courage, not despair; growth, not death.

The fact that some claim far too much for the science of behavior is no reason to claim too little. As you make your way through your first course, always keep the complexity of behavior in mind—not as an obstacle but as a challenge. It is also a constant reminder that superficial ideas will not provide explanations, and superficial methods of helping will not change really important human behaviors.

It is our conviction that after close to a century of research, the scientific knowledge of human behavior is extremely limited. You can look upon these limitations as sources of frustration, which prevent you from understanding yourself and others. Or you can look upon these limitations as challenges to explore beyond the frontiers of our knowledge, to go beyond the known into unknown territories. People have been trying for centuries to understand behavior. They have for all those centuries used many different, nonscientific approaches to knowledge. Perhaps using science in addition to the other methods will bring major new understanding of those unexplored territories.

The search provides a kind of satisfaction that we cannot describe adequately. One way for you to get a taste of that satisfaction is to discover for yourself what is already known. That is, to come to terms with the knowledge in your psychology course with a spirit of healthy skepticism and inquiry. By *skepticism* we mean a demand for evidence. By *inquiry* we mean *asking questions about behavior.*

References

Appley, M., & Trumbull, R. (Eds.). *Psychological stress: issues in research*. New York: Appleton-Century-Crofts, 1967.

Bahnsen, C. B. Emotional reactions to internally and externally derived threat of annihilation. In G. H. Grosser, H. Wechsler, & M. Greenblatt (Eds.), *The threat of impending disaster: contributions to the psychology of stress*. Cambridge, Massachusetts: M.I.T. Press, 1964.

Balke, W. M., Hammond, K. R., & Meyer, G. D. An alternate approach to labor-management relations. *Administrative Science Quarterly*, September 1973, **18**(3), 311–28. Reprinted by permission.

Bandura, A. *Principles of behavior modification*. New York: Holt, Rinehart and Winston, 1969.

Basowitz, H., Persky, H., Korchin, S. J., & Grinker, R. R. *Anxiety and stress*. New York: McGraw-Hill, 1955.

Bergin, A. E., & Garfield, S. L. (Eds.). *Handbook of psychotherapy and behavior change: an empirical analysis*. New York: Wiley, 1971.

Biderman, A. D. Captivity lore and behavior in captivity. In G. H. Grosser, H. Wechsler, & M. Greenblatt (Eds.), *The threat of impending disaster: contributions to the psychology of stress*. Cambridge, Massachusetts: M.I.T. Press, 1964.

Brady, J. V. Ulcers in "executive monkeys." *Scientific American*, 1958, **199,** 95–103. Reprinted by permission.

Breger, L. The ideology of behaviorism. In L. Breger (Ed.), *Clinical-cognitive psychology: models and integrations*. Englewood Cliffs, New Jersey: Prentice-Hall, 1969.

Broadbent, D. E. *Decision and stress*. New York: Academic Press, 1971.

Budzynski, T. H., Stoyva, J. M., & Adler, C. S. Feedback-induced muscle relaxation: application to tension headache. Paper presented at ninth annual meeting of the Society for Psychophysiological Research, Monterey, California, October 1969. Published in *Journal of Behavior Therapy and Experimental Psychiatry*, 1970, **1**(3).

Budzynski, T. H., Stoyva, J. M., Adler, C. S., & Mullaney, D. J. EMG biofeedback and tension headache: a controlled outcome study. *Psychosomatic Medicine*, 1973, **35,** 484–96. Reprinted by permission.

Cannon, W. B. "Voodoo" death. *American Anthropologist*, 1942, **44,** 169–81. Reproduced by permission of the American Anthropological Association.

Coelho, G. V., Hamburg, D. A., & Adams, J. E. (Eds.). *Coping and adaptation.* New York: Basic Books, 1974.

Davidson, G. C. Systematic desensitization as a counterconditioning process. *Journal of Abnormal Psychology*, 1968, **73,** 91–99.

DesLauriers, A. M., & Carlson, C. F. *Your child is asleep: early infantile autism.* Homewood, Illinois: Dorsey, 1969.

Eron, L. D. Relationship of TV viewing habits and aggressive behavior in children. *Journal of Abnormal and Social Psychology*, 1963, **67,** 193–96.

Eron, L. D., Huesmann, L. R., Lefkowitz, M. M., & Walder, L. O. Does television violence cause aggression? *American Psychologist*, 1972, **27,** 253–63.

Eron, L. D., Walder, L. O., & Lefkowitz, M. M. *Learning of aggression in children.* Boston: Little Brown and Company, 1971. Reprinted by permission of the authors. (This book is currently available from Pergamon Press, Inc., Maxwell House, Fairview Park, Elmsford, New York 10523.)

Geen, R. G. *Personality, the skein of behavior.* St. Louis, Missouri: C. V. Mosby, 1976.

Ginott, H. G. *Group psychotherapy with children: the theory and practice of play therapy.* New York: McGraw-Hill, 1961.

Glass, D. C., & Singer, J. E. *Urban stress: experiments on noise and social stressors.* New York: Academic Press, 1972.

Grinker, R. R., & Spiegel, J. *Men under stress.* Philadelphia: Blakiston, 1945.

Haley, J. Family therapy. In A. M. Freedman, H. I. Kaplan, & B. J. Sadock (Eds.), *Comprehensive textbook of psychiatry* (2nd. ed., vol. II). Baltimore: Williams & Wilkins, 1975.

Haney, C., Banks, C., & Zimbardo, P. Interpersonal dynamics in a simulated prison. *International Journal of Criminology and Penology*, 1973, **1,** 69–97.

Harrison, S. I. Child psychiatry: psychiatric treatment. In A. M. Freedman, H. I. Kaplan, & B. J. Sadock (Eds.), *Comprehensive textbook of psychiatry* (2nd ed., vol. II). Baltimore: Williams & Wilkins, 1975.

Hebb, D. O. *The organization of behavior.* New York: Wiley, 1949.

Hunt, J. McV. The effects of infant feeding frustration upon adult hoarding behavior in the albino rat. *Journal of Abnormal and Social Psychology,* 1941, **36,** 338–60.

Johnson, H. J. Decision making, conflict, and physiological arousal. *Journal of Abnormal and Social Psychology,* 1963, **67**(2), 114–24.

Kahn, R. L., Wolfe, D. M., Quinn, R. P., & Snoek, J. D. *Organizational stress.* New York: Wiley, 1964.

Lazarus, R. S. A laboratory approach to the dynamics of psychological stress. In G. H. Grosser, H. Wechsler, & M. Greenblatt (Eds.), *The threat of impending disaster: contributions to the psychology of stress.* Cambridge, Massachusetts: M.I.T. Press, 1964.

Liebert, R. M., & Baron, R. A. Some immediate effects of television violence on children's behavior. *Developmental Psychology,* 1972, **6,** 469–75.

Lifton, R. J. Psychological effects of the atomic bomb in Hiroshima: the theme of death. In G. H. Grosser, H. Wechsler, & M. Greenblatt (Eds.), *The threat of impending disaster: contributions to the psychology of stress.* Cambridge, Massachusetts: M.I.T. Press, 1964.

Marx, M. H., & Goodson, F. E. (Eds.). *Theories in contemporary psychology.* New York: Macmillan, 1976.

Masserman, J. H. *Behavior and neuroses.* Chicago: University of Chicago Press, 1943. Copyright 1943 by The University of Chicago. Reprinted by permission.

McGrath, J. E. Stress and behavior in organizations. In M. D. Dunnette (Ed.). *Handbook of industrial and organizational psychology.* Chicago: Rand McNally, 1976.

Milgram, S. *Obedience to authority: an experimental view.* New York: Harper & Row, 1974.

Miller, N. Studies of fear as an acquirable drive: I. fear as motivation and fear as reinforcement in the learning of new responses. *Journal of Experimental Psychology,* 1948, **38,** 89–100.

Miller, N. E., & DiCara, L. V. Instrumental learning of heart rate changes in curarized rats: shaping and specificity to discriminative stimulus. *Journal of Comparative and Physiological Psychology,* 1967, **63,** 12–19.

Miller, N. E., & Dworkin, B. R. Visceral learning: recent difficulties with curarized rats and significant problems for human research. In P. A. Obrist, A. H. Black, J. Brener, & L. V. DiCara (Eds.), *Cardiovascular Psychophysiology.* Chicago: Aldine, 1974.

Neisser, U. *Cognition and reality.* San Francisco:W. H. Freeman, 1976.

Patterson, G. R. Behavioral techniques based upon social learning: an additional base for developing behavior modification technologies. In C. M. Franks (Ed.), *Behavior therapy, appraisal & status.* New York: McGraw-Hill, 1969.

Radloff, R., & Helmreich, R. *Groups under stress: psychological research in Sealab II.* New York: Appleton-Century-Crofts, 1968.

Ruff, G. E., & Korchin, S. J. Psychological responses of the Mercury astronauts to stress. In G. H. Grosser, H. Wechsler, & M. Greenblatt (Eds.), *The threat of impending disaster: contributions to the psychology of stress.* Cambridge, Massachusetts: M.I.T. Press, 1964.

Sadock, V. Marital therapy. In A. M. Freedman, H. I. Kaplan, & B. J. Sadock (Eds.), *Comprehensive textbook of psychiatry* (2nd ed., vol. II). Baltimore: Williams & Wilkins, 1975.

Sarason, S. B., Davidson, K. S., Lighthall, F. F., Waite, R. R., & Ruebush, B. K. *Anxiety in elementary school children.* New Haven, Connecticut: Yale University Press, 1960.

Schachter, S. *The psychology of affiliation.* Stanford, California: Stanford University Press, 1959. Pp. 13–15 and 21 reprinted by permission of Stanford University Press.

Selye, H. *The stress of life* (Rev. ed.). New York: McGraw-Hill, 1976.

Shurley, J. T. Profound experimental sensory isolation. *American Journal of Psychiatry,* 1960, **117,** 539–45. Copyright 1960, The American Psychiatric Association. Reprinted by permission.

Shurley, J. T. Hallucinations in sensory deprivation and sleep deprivation. In L. J. West (Ed.), *Hallucinations.* New York: Grune & Stratton, 1962.

Silverman, I., & Geer, J. H. The elimination of a recurrent nightmare by desensitization of a related phobia. *Behaviour Research and Therapy,* 1968, **6,** 109–11. Reprinted by permission of Pergamon Press Ltd.

Skinner, B. F. A case history in scientific method. In S. Koch (Ed.), *Psychology: a study of a science* (Vol. 2). New York: McGraw-Hill, 1959.

Spock, B. *Baby and child care.* New York: Pocket Books, 1957.

Suedfeld, P. The benefits of boredom: sensory deprivation reconsidered. *American Scientist,* 1975, **63,** 60–69.

Toch, H. *Men in crisis: human breakdowns in prisons.* Chicago: Aldine, 1975.

Weiss, J. M. Effects of coping responses on stress. *Journal of Comparative and Physiological Psychology,* 1968, **65,** 251–60.

Wolberg, L. R. *The technique of psychotherapy* (2nd ed., vols. I & II). New York: Grune & Stratton, 1967.

Wolf, M. M., Risley, T. R., & Mees, H. L. Application of operant conditioning procedures to the behavior problems of an autistic child. *Behaviour Research and Therapy,* 1964, **1,** 305–312. Reprinted by permission of Pergamon Press Ltd.

Yalom, I. D. *The theory and practice of group psychotherapy.* New York: Basic Books, 1970.